IRISH LIFE AND LORE SERIES

THE PREMIER COUNTY OF
TIPPERARY

LIVING VOICES

Text by JANE O'HEA O'KEEFFE
Recordings compiled and edited by MAURICE O'KEEFFE

Privately published by Maurice O'Keeffe & Jane O'Hea O'Keeffe
2006

Printed by KINGDOM PRINTERS LTD.
TRALEE, CO. KERRY. *Tel:* 066 7121136

Printed June 2006

ISBN 0-9543274-7-0

For our children Helene, Claire, and David, with thanks for all the support and
encouragement, but particulary for all the laughter and the love.

ACKNOWLEDGEMENTS

We wish to thank sincerely all the gracious participants in these recordings. Their good humour, patience, co-operation and hospitality made our work a real pleasure, and for this we are very grateful.

Particular thanks are due to Breda Cleary and Siobhan Geraghty, Joe Rea, Maura O'Brien, George Cunningham, Dom Laurence Walsh OCSO, William Hayes and Sister Placida Barry.

We must also thank Nora Burke, our typist for all her care and attention, Kieran Mc Carthy of Kingdom Printers for his expertise and patience, and Core Media Distribution for their professional production of the recordings.

The complete collection of 45 recordings or any individual recording may be obtained by contacting: Maurice & Jane O'Keeffe
                            Ballyroe, Tralee, Co. Kerry.
                            066 7121991
or through website: www.irishlifeandlore.com
                            email: okeeffeantiques2@eircom.net
Individual cd's: €20
Complete collection of 45 cd's: €800

Previous Books written by Jane O'Hea O'Keeffe and published in the Irish Life & Lore Series of books and recordings:

The Ancient Barony of Duhallow - Living Voices

Recollections of 1916 and its Aftermath - Echoes from History

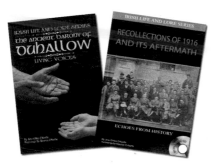

INTRODUCTION

It has been a real pleasure for me to work on this book over the last two years. To listen to the voices of Tipperary is to experience a profound sense of history, of belonging and of pride.

The absolute sense of rootedness in the soil of the county and the honesty and openness of the voices combine to make the past come alive once again, while enfolding the cold facts of history in a warm human embrace.

Our rich and vibrant oral history cannot be compared with documented history, with all its professional technicality and restriction, but oral history alone can access the variety and complexity of the unique human memory. The varied cadences of the recorded voices help to illustrate and to enrich the differing perspectives on the local history of the county. Our oral tradition opens the portals to the past in a colourful and vibrant recounting of personal recollection, interspersed with great music, recitation and song.

I am extremely conscious of the hospitality and courtesy shown to my husband Maurice as he recorded the people featured in this book, and to myself as I worked on the text. We hope that our work will help to provide an arena in which the voices of the county of Tipperary may be shared, enjoyed, studied, preserved and honoured.

Jane O'Hea O'Keeffe
Tralee, Co. Kerry.
June 2006

Collections of Recordings in the "Irish Life & Lore Series".

Collection I - 120 CDs - Kerry & Clare - 2002

Collection II - 213 CDs - North Cork, West Limerick, Galway & Kerry - 2004

Collection III - 33 CDs - Recollection of 1916 - 2005

Collection IV - 54 CDs - North Kerry - 2005

Collection V - 45 CDs - Tipperary - 2006

Collection VI - 12 CDs - Kerry (Archieves in Profile) - 2005

www.irishlifeandlore.com

FOREWORD

The Irish Life and Lore series of recordings are unique and of lasting and primary importance. Indeed, I know of no other ongoing project which adds as much to our heritage, as do these recordings of the oral traditions of our land.

This Tipperary Collection, consisting of 45 recordings, adds another rich layer to those published on Kerry, Clare, Cork, Limerick and Galway. In all, over 900 recordings of prime historical material, most of which would have been lost without the initiative and sheer hard work of Maurice and Jane O'Keeffe. Now to add to the recordings, Jane has researched and edited this attractive, accompanying book; added value at its best!

The Tipperary Collection (Limerick and Offaly people will forgive the slight annexation of their territories) is as diverse as it is eclectic in its locations, raconteurs and subject matters, the oral memorabilia of everyday life and yesterday's riches. Clichéd though the phrase may be, all human life is here, and how entertaining it all is. In the recordings, with an easy deceptive laidback style, Maurice brings out the best in his interviewees, monks and farmers, historians and nuns, teachers and housewives, to mention just a few; and in this lovely gem of a book Jane, also with a simple but very effective flowing narrative, paints the background that allows us almost to eavesdrop as each recording is made.

We had the pleasure, at a recent Roscrea conference at Mount St Joseph Cistercian Abbey, of having the initial launch of the Tipperary Collection – a fitting place, indeed, for many reasons, not least that two of the contributors are monks of Roscrea. And just how timely and important Maurice's work is, may be gauged by the fact that shortly after he recorded Brother Peter, his gentle soul went to his heavenly reward.

I am honoured and proud to be part of the collection, doubly so as I talk about my favourite place on this earth, Monaincha, the 31st Wonder of the World. As Maurice and Jane keep going, moving into different Irish counties to record ordinary and not-so-ordinary people, their work will truly become one of the wonders of modern Ireland.

Rath De orthu.
George Cunningham,
Roscrea.
1st June 2006

Tom Ryan, Ballinree House, Cashel, Co Tipperary

CD No. 1
Time: 46.26
Date Recorded: August 2005

The warm summer air was filled with the loud and raucous clamour of crows as I arrived at Ballinree House on an August evening in 2005, to meet my gracious host Tom Ryan. This lovely old estate house was built by the Smith-Barry family of Fota House, Cork, in 1852. In January 1849 the estate was home to 470 people and by the summer of that year only 47 people remained, as a result of the drastic policy of clearance employed by the landlord in those days.

By the early 1850s the estate was being run as a commercial farm, and in 1908 John Bryant, who was grandfather to the present owner, became estate manager, a position he held until 1926 when Lord Barrymore died and the Land Commission divided up the estate. The Bryant family then acquired the present house.

Tom Ryan and I stood in the old farmyard, and my eye was caught by a weighing scale, which had obviously stood sentinel here for generations. Tom described how all produce leaving the estate in the old days had to be weighed, including corn destined for the grain merchants in Thurles, and cattle which were driven on foot to Cashel. On one occasion, a complaint was made in Cashel that the weight of the cattle on arrival differed from that specified on leaving Ballinree. Mr Bryant had the cattle weighed again in Cashel and discovered that the herd had lost four stone in weight having walked the six miles from Ballinree to the town.

All the sheds around the farmyard are slated, and the walls are decorated with a shamrock, a symbol used by the Smith-Barry family. Tom described the fascinating system used to feed the animals. A platform runs around the outside walls of the sheds, and little carriages would run on a railway track laid on the platform. The carriages, powered by two horses, would run beneath the turnip pulper, and then be tipped into troughs for feeding – an early and efficient labour saving system.

Our journey next took us past a fine old gate, made by the original estate blacksmith, and I was then confronted by the sight of a magnificent Bowl Barrow, built on the highest ground for miles around. At its centre is a burial chamber and small cist graves are inserted into the sides of the mound. The Barrow measures eight to nine feet in height and fifty feet in diameter and dates from around 3,500 BC.

Travelling in a south easterly direction from the Barrow we walked down to view the Standing Stone which is now lying flat on the ground. This would most likely have originally stood on the Barrow and Tom pointed out that the Stone could not have been quarried within a half mile of its present position and it begs the intriguing question – how was it transported to this elevated place?

On our return journey to the house I spotted the remains of a beautiful old stone wall, surrounding the original kitchen garden which encompassed eight acres. One old apple tree survives and recently the people from 'Seed Savers' were thrilled to discover it, as this variety of apple – 'Davy' – has not been known to exist in Ireland for over forty years.

Tom named for me all the important employees of the old estate and I was delighted to hear that descendants of the blacksmith, herdsman, shepherd and the carters still live in the locality.

Back in the farmyard, I admired the relic of an old 1949 Ferguson tractor, which prompted Tom to recall an eerie story about the fate of a pair of horses which were put to work by Tom's uncle cutting hay in a fort nearby.

I was filled with admiration at the ingenuity of the engineers of earlier days, as Tom explained to me the system used to pipe water to the house from a river two miles away. He also showed me the pipes used to pump hot water into the greenhouse to keep the temperature warm, and the plants thriving.

The crows had settled down for the night as I left Ballinree House, a place filled with a sense of history and continuity, and as I bade farewell to Tom Ryan, I recognised how privileged I had been to have seen such a wonderful place, so steeped in history and to have heard its fascinating story.

Philip Ryan, Boherlahan, Cashel, Co Tipperary

CD No. 2
Time: 48.56
Date Recorded: August 2005

On a warm August day in 2005, I made my way to the home of Philip Ryan of Boherlahan, near Cashel. Once I had been welcomed warmly and well, Philip showed me a photograph of the old Boherlahan School which was built in the years after 1830. Philip began his teaching career here in 1948 and continued on that path of dedication for forty years, until his retirement as Principal in 1988. He was preceeded as Principal by a Mr Kennedy who began teaching in 1904, and prior to this the Principal of the school was William Ryan, whose career began here in 1860.

Philip proudly pointed out that his granduncle, Billy Moloney, a classical scholar, had taught in the Hedge School at Thurlesbeg. Another relative, Edmund Delaney had taught in the school in 1846, and according to an entry in the old school records for that period, there were seventy to eighty pupils on the roll though only twenty to thirty children attended school on any given day. These were famine times, filled with hunger, hardship and grief.

When I enquired how teachers were taught in those days, Philip explained that when the National Schools began in 1830, the monitor system came into play, whereby bright children who had reached an age to finish primary school were retained at the school to help the teacher and to receive further education in maths, English, Irish and the Classics. After three to four years as a monitor they qualified for training college and eventually became teachers.

The Primary School Curriculum consisted of the 3 Rs and some Latin and Greek, important languages in the Catholic Church which was so strong and powerful at this time. Local boys who showed an aptitude for learning were strongly encouraged to join the priesthood.

Philip's primary school education began in Ardmayle and he remembers his teachers fondly – Mr Jim O'Brien and Miss Kennedy. Irish was always his favourite subject and when he began his secondary education in Cashel he found his standard of Irish to be at least two years ahead of the standard being taught there. When he began his primary teaching career in 1948 the system of teaching and the curriculum had changed little since his own schooldays, but in the 1960s a new curriculum was introduced, which included Physical Education. He recalls attending a lecture at that time, on the teaching of PE. A friend of his, Jim Sheridan, who taught in Dualla, relating to him that an entry appeared in an Inspector's Report on the school in Dualla in earlier days, stating that a teacher had been found teaching the children outdoors, about birds, animals and nature and the Inspector's entry noted that "this was all very well, but was not part of the curriculum."

Philip Ryan always loved the stories and legends of old Ireland, and had no difficulty in reciting, in Irish, lines from these stories and also the first few lines of Goldsmith's *The Deserted Village*.

We had a discussion on corporal punishment in schools in former days, and Philip is strong in his assertion that it was never a good thing. However, he does maintain that discipline is always a problem in schools, but feels that corporal punishment was never the correct response. He has always had a love of local history and was very pleased recently to have been asked by the local teacher to take some school children, including his own grandson, to see the grave of Charles Bianconi at Boherlahan, and to Ardmayle to view the remains of the 12th century Norman church there.

We spoke of place names in the locality, including Irish names which are descriptive of a ruined castle at Ardmayle, a wide road, St Brigid's Well or the pilgrim's well, Nodstown and the Black Heather. I learned of a townland locally which won three All-Ireland hurling medals in 1895, 1896 and 1898 and Philip assured me that within the boundaries of that townland there are 50 All-Ireland medals resulting from these famous victories.

Both of Philip Ryan's grandfathers were involved in the setting up of Ardmayle Co-op Creamery in 1899, which thrived until its amalgamation with Mitchelstown Co-op in 1972. His father was also a committee member and Philip himself was secretary for some years.

The old school at Boherlahan

As I prepared to take my leave, Philip told me something which brought a powerful image to mind. On his first day at school, he was accompanied by a young boy who was to become a legendary Tipperary man, T. J. Maher, one time Head of the IFA and a member of the European Parliament for 15 years. They grew up together as neighbours and as I drove away, the powerful image of the young Mr Maher taking the infant Mr Ryan by the hand to begin his most fruitful journey towards learning, guidance and teaching, was as clear and distinct as the road before me.

Chrissie Ryan-Coole, Coolnacalla, Newport, Co Tipperary

CD No. 3
Time: 45.00
Date Recorded: July 2005

My good friend, Patrick Humphries suggested to me that I might interview Chrissie Ryan-Coole of Coolnacalla, as he felt she would have some great reminiscences to share. During the summer of 2005 I made my way to Chrissie's home and was graciously invited to sit with her by her warm fire, and listen to her story.

Chrissie is now in her nineties and is somewhat hard of hearing, but this detracted in no way from our delving into her wealth of memories. She was born in December 1914, the same month in which her future husband Pat first saw the light. Her maiden name was Ahern and she had an older sister, Mary. I asked Chrissie to tell me about the generations of Ryans who had lived in the house, and she named three former Mrs Ryans. Some of the Ryan land had been sold in a previous generation but happily had later been purchased back by the family, some of it after a lapse of 70 years. As a young child she remembers seeing the light from the flames which consumed the creamery at Newport during the frightful reign of the Black and Tans.

During the Civil War, a neighbour, Bridgie O'Grady would regularly bake nine cakes of bread to feed the boys on the run. On one occasion, the Free State Soldiers came to the house and asked for food to be cooked for them. Bridgie was frightened by one man who kept clicking his gun, so she asked Ned to come in from the yard. He told the soldier to come outside with his gun and they'd see who was the better man. The Officer in Charge apologised to Bridgie for the soldier's behaviour, peace was restored and tensions released.

We spoke of the Economic War of the 1930s and the many hardships endured by farming people. Chrissie maintained that people had to be self sufficient or they would not have survived and there were very many desperately poor people in the locality in those days. She told the story of a neighbour who brought firkins of butter to Limerick to be sold, and got £40 for his product, which was a great amount of money. He sat on a window to rest and the money was stolen from him. On returning home he told his wife who was distraught. She walked all the long miles to Limerick in the hope that the money could be found, but needless to say, she had no luck and returned home in utter despair.

When Chrissie was ten years old and her sister Mary was 16, their mother died, and their father then had to struggle to bring up his two daughters alone. There was not a lot of organised entertainment locally in those days, but dances were a huge attraction for the young people. Unfortunately these events were not always blessed by the local priests and sermons were given from the pulpit about the evils of such dances. Chrissie also recalled that as her father was fairly strict, it was not always easy to get to the social gatherings but she has great memories of the entertainment at the hall at Newport.

She had some fascinating stories to relate about superstitions and pisheogs, in which she firmly believes, and I found myself in thrall to the tales of good and evil which figured so prominently in the lives of our ancestors.

The time had come to go and I was reluctant to take my leave of this great lady who so generously and warmly shared with me the story of her long and fruitful life.

Maura O'Brien, Dualla, Cashel, Co Tipperary

CD No. 4
Time: 35.05
Date Recorded: September 2005

On a September day in 2005, I knocked on the door of Maura O'Brien's home at Dualla, and I was very pleased indeed to meet the lady of the house. Once we had settled ourselves and begun to talk, Maura told me that she had made some tape recordings in the 1980s during various get-togethers and birthday parties for her mother and two aunts who lived in the house and who have all now passed away.

I was most interested to hear of this and asked to hear a recording, so one of the tapes was set to play and such a feast of chat and music filled the room. One of Maura's aunts, Mary Finn, nee Ryan, went to school in Belgium for a period. This was organised by her cousin, Mother de Sales Lowry in Waterford, an influential woman who introduced the Montessori system of teaching to Ireland.

Mary's sister Katie was a wonderful singer and was a member of the local choir for over sixty years. From a tape dated July 1985 we listened to the company in the house give a fine rendition of *Slievenamon* and *The Old Bog Road* accompanied by accordion player John Buckley from Clonmel.

As I listened to the tape I discussed with Maura the fact that music and singing have always formed such an important part of any social gathering in Ireland, be it a wedding or a wake, and especially the American wakes of old.

As the singing came to an end, somebody says clearly "It's 10.30, time to go to bed," so that tape came to a conclusion shortly afterwards to the sounds of the guests preparing to take their leave.

I then chatted to Maura about her own life as a teacher, and her years spent caring for her mother, aunts and uncles. She described those years, getting up each morning at 6.30 a.m in her house in Cashel, in order to get breakfast for her mother and then for her aunts in Dualla, get to school and to visit her aunts again later in the day. Her mother died in 1985 and Maura then lived with her aunts, caring for them for one and a half years until both of these elderly ladies died within four weeks of one another.

Another tape was set to play, and we listened with amusement as Maura's mother, Ellen O'Brien tells a great story about an old West Cork woman who went on a trip to Cork city to sell a basket of eggs. It was a telling tale involving a country man who left his origins far behind when he went to work in the city! Before I left, Maura recited for me a poem written by her uncle Jack Ryan in 1981. It is entitled *Happy Memories* and is set in the house of William Laffan in Dualla.

I was filled with admiration as I pondered on the caring and nurturing nature of Maura O'Brien's full life, and I was very pleased to have been afforded the opportunity to listen to the voices and laughter of her relatives who have now gone to their final reward.

The late Katie Ryan, Maura O'Brien and the late Mary Finn.

The late Mother de Sales.

Catherine Mc Auley

CD No. 5
Time: 32.44
Date Recorded: September 2005

While sitting in the kitchen of Maura O'Brien's home in Dualla, in which her mother's family the Ryans, have lived since 1870, I asked Maura about the origins of the place name. She told me she felt the word meant 'Kelly's Land' as there was another area close by called Ballykelly.

Prior to the Ryan family inhabiting the old house, it had been owned by the Skehans and earlier still by Philip Meagher, who was married to a lady named Sheehy. Her cousin was Fr Sheehy, who, as a student was kept in hiding in the house during the Penal days.

Maura O'Brien has always had an interest in the religious orders, and when one of the teachers in Cashel suggested she write an article on local women who entered the religious life, Maura began her research. Her first article for the local journal was submitted in 2003. I asked her how she went about her research and was told that she visited the families of the sisters initially and she also wrote to the convents requesting information from their archives, having first said a prayer to Mary Potter, Nano Nagle and Mother McAuley. The prayers were answered and the information began to flow.

Maura was fascinated to discover that eight girls from a local road which stretched for only one mile had entered the Little Sisters of Mary, also known as the Blue Nuns. The order was founded by Mary Potter who was born in London in 1847 to non-Catholic parents. Her mother became a Catholic and had her children baptised into the Catholic Church. As a young woman Mary became engaged, but having read a book about Our Lady she changed her mind and went on to found the Order, which was dedicated to caring for the poor, the sick and the dying. Maura told me that three O'Neill sisters from the locality entered the religious life as did girls from the Ryan and O'Dwyer families.

The story of Nano Nagle, the founder of the Presentation Order was most interesting to hear. Nano was born in Mallow, the oldest of seven children. Her family were well-to-do and she was sent to France to further her education. One morning, as she was returning home from a party, she spotted a group of poverty stricken people waiting to attend early Mass. This image haunted her for six years, and on her return home to Ireland she was appalled at the poverty she witnessed. With her brother's help she set up her first school in Cork. She died in 1865.

Mother McAuley, founder of the Mercy Sisters, was a Dublin woman and when her parents died while the family were still very young, the children were cared for by relatives. She was later sent to work for a Quaker family named Callaghan, and she inherited their estate upon their demise. This enabled her to start a school and a refuge for destitute women and children in Baggot Street in Dublin.

I was told an amazing story about Sister Ignatius Maher, who was buried at sea, and I heard that the grave of lay sister Martha Moloney, who was born in 1846 was visited by people in times of illness.

I left Maura O'Brien's house in Dualla with my head filled with information about these courageous and unselfish women whose stories have now been preserved due to the interest and dedication of a lady who realises the importance of retaining the tenuous link between the past and the present day.

Breda Tierney at age 6. Photographed by Fr. F. Browne SJ 1940
(©Fr. Francis Browne SJ Collection)

CD No. 6
Time: 30.55
Date Recorded: September 2005

Historians are familiar with the name of Colonel Jack O'Farrell, who acted as ADC to William T. Cosgrave in the 1920s and who had been present on that momentous day in 1921 when the Anglo Irish Treaty was signed in London. In the autumn of 2005, I was delighted to be introduced to Breda Tierney, who is a daughter of Col O'Farrell. I met Breda at the home of Maura O'Brien at Dualla, and sat enthralled to listen to her recollections of her father.

She told me that though Col O'Farrell had lived through dangerous and historic days in Ireland, he was always reluctant to speak of those times, but she was happy to share with me the recollections she had of him and the details he did disclose to his family. Jack O'Farrell was with Michael Collins and several others in the Kildare Street club on the night before Collins began his fateful journey to West Cork in August 1922. They all wore trilby raincoats and before leaving the club that night Collins helped Col O'Farrell into his coat and said "See you on Thursday night Jack", a promise which fate determined he was never to keep.

Col O'Farrell was among the significant group which had in the previous year travelled to London for the signing of the Treaty. Once the documents were signed Collins stood up and turning to his right he spoke to Col O'Farrell who was standing behind him, and said, "Now Jack, remember this. Your children and their children, and their children's children will never see peace in Ireland." Col O'Farrell was later to assist Dr Gogarty to embalm the body of his friend and comrade in the Meath Hospital after the fatal shot was fired at Béal na Bláth.

Breda Tierney asked her father on his deathbed who had shot Collins. She recalls that there was a Sacred Heart picture hanging on the bedroom wall. Her father rested his eyes on the picture for a moment, looked at his daughter and said, "It's best that I take that information to the grave with me."

A fascinating historical detail came to light during the story of the kidnapping of Senator Bagwell, Director of the Great Southern Railways. He was located in the Wicklow mountains, rescued, and Col O'Farrell was entrusted with the task of accompanying him to England and safety. The two men, dressed as women for the journey, arrived safely at the Dorchester Hotel in London, where Senator Begwell, unsurprisingly, suffered a breakdown as a result of his horrendous experiences and insisted that Col O'Farrell should not leave him. Breda smiled as she imagined her father at about 24 years of age, swanning around the luxurious surroundings of the Dorchester Hotel over the following six weeks, without a care in the world.

She showed me some historically important photographs featuring her father, and a charming photograph taken by the famous photographer Fr Frank Browne in 1940. The photograph features in the book *Fr Browne's Ireland,* above the caption 'Swinging on the pump at Leighlinbridge (1940)' and the little swinger on the pump is the young Breda herself.

I then drew Maura O'Brien into the conversation and we discussed the customs in the countryside in days gone by. Maura's house saw many a great social gathering. Her mother remembered counting 60 people in the house on one occasion, all of whom were being fed, to the accompaniment of music, singing, dancing and recitation.

Maura recalled the open fire, the crane and skillet pot, the butter boxes used as seats at milking time, and also used for sitting comfortably by the warm fire at night. Everybody was self sufficient, making their own bread, growing vegetables and potatoes, rearing and killing pigs. Maura's mother would have four pigs killed each year, and Maura would be sent to the cousins and neighbours with the pork steaks and the puddings.

I enjoyed those wonderful few hours in Dualla with two great ladies who generously and willingly recalled for me the light, the laughter and indeed the tragedies of other days in Tipperary.

Father Nivard Kinsella OCSO, Mount St Joseph Cistercian Abbey, Roscrea, Co Tipperary

CD No. 7
Time: 54.00
Date Recorded: October 2005

Over the years I have attended many of the spring and autumn conferences at Mount St Joseph Cistercian Abbey in Roscrea, and as I drive in through the imposing gates and up the winding driveway, I always look forward to a warm and hearty welcome by Fr Nivard Kinsella, who is guestmaster at the Abbey.

On my most recent visit in October 2005, my wife Jane and I were invited to launch the Tipperary Collection of 45 recordings in the "Irish Life and Lore Series". Once that pleasant task was accomplished, I settled down in the parlour with Fr Nivard to listen to his story and to his reflections on his life as a Cistercian monk.

Fr Nivard was born in Rathgar in Dublin, attended the Christian Brothers School at Westland Row, and later St Mary's Rathmines. Each year his father would come to Mount St Joseph Abbey on Retreat, and would talk to his son about it on his return. During Nivard's last year at school, he came to see the place for himself, liked it, and having completed his Leaving Certificate, entered the monastery. He later spent a couple of years in Australia and worked on his Doctorate in Theology in Rome for three years.

I learned that the Cistercian Order was founded in 1098 in France and Mount Mellary was founded in Waterford in 1832. Then in 1875 a wealthy Catholic MP for South Tipperary, Arthur Moore, approached the Abbot of Mount Mellary to offer to underwrite the purchase of a house in South Tipperary, near Roscrea, to found a monastery there. This was agreed and the house and 200 acres were acquired for £15,000, Arthur Moore writing off £5,000 of the debt. A community of twelve monks came initially to live and work there from Mount Mellary. In 1880 work began on the building of the Church with stone quarried from the lands and the church was opened in 1883. In 1936 the magnificent spire was built.

Nivard explained to me that when he entered the Order rules were very strictly enforced. The monks never spoke without permission from the Abbot, and would communicate by symbols and signs. This was designed to restrict communication and as Nivard said, was somewhat unrealistic for adults in their daily lives. Also, in the older tradition, the monks would rise at 2.00 a.m. for office at 2.15 a.m. each morning. Now office is said at 4.00 a.m. and Compline at 7.30 p.m. or 8.00 p.m., depending on the season.

Discipline becomes second nature after a time, and a monk's day is punctuated by prayer and work. When Nivard first entered the Order it was to be 10 years before he felt the need to go outside the gates. In those early days there were 18 horses and one tractor to work the farm, nowadays there are 4 tractors and no horses. One dearly loved member of the Community, Br Peter, who died in 2005 at the age of 97, always preferred to use a donkey rather than a horse while working on the farm as he felt a donkey was "much better for contemplation."

Our conversation ranged over many and varied topics including holy wells and pattern days, the Penitential Pilgrimages to Lough Derg, the tradition of fasting, the necessity of a sense of humour and the great concept of loneliness. We spoke of the boarding school which was set up here in 1905, partly due to the donation of the inheritance of Arthur Moore's son who was killed in a riding accident. There are now 300 boarders at the school, who come from all over Ireland.

We discussed the immense changes which have come about in Ireland over the past few decades and Fr Nivard maintained that change must be accepted in the Church as in all things. His only regret is the emergence of the consumer society but "to live is to change" he says with conviction.

The church bell began to toll as I took my leave of Mount St Joseph Abbey and as I thanked Fr Nivard for his courtesy and his kindness, the great sense of peace and reflection which pervades this place descended upon me as I began my long journey homeward.

Peter Read, Old Castle House, Roscrea, Co Tipperary

CD No. 8
Time: 74.27
Date Recorded: October 2003

On a brisk and bracing day in October 2003 I made my way to Old Castle House, which is situated in the grounds of the O'Carroll settlement near the town of Roscrea. Here I was greeted by the charming owner, Peter Read, who brought me into his study, a veritable archive of his family's history. A most fascinating and absorbing couple of hours ensued.

Peter began by outlining the history of the Castle, a tower house built in 1640, and inhabited on a continual basis until it was burnt in 1921. The castle was roofed when the present house was built in the early part of the 20th century, so happily, deterioration to the structure of the castle has been minimal since that time.

The Read family have had a long and happy association with nearby Mount St Joseph Cistercian Monastery, and Peter fondly recalls Fr William, who at one time decided to design a grain drying machine. On the day of its unveiling, Fr William, with bated breath, fired it up, but the great event came to an abrupt conclusion when smoke began to billow from the machine and it became engulfed in flames.

The Read family of Roscrea have always been involved in milling, and Peter Read is the proud owner of the last four bottles of Roscrea Whiskey bottled in 1914 by Smiths of Rosemary Square, and bonded in the Roscrea Bond Store. These bottles now hold pride of place in his study. The family also had a keen interest in shipping. Dr Edward Watson, who married Peter's aunt, founded the City of Dublin Steam Company, which was involved in mail delivery to Holyhead. Standing proudly in Peter's study is a model of the paddle steamer 'Ireland' which transported mails, and as he removed the decking of the model I was amazed to see below deck a series of postal sorting boxes. The mails would be sorted during the trip to Holyhead and be ready for distribution on arrival.

The model had been badly broken up in earlier years, and as I admired Peter's craftsmanship in restoring it to its present excellent condition he told me that he had been trained in carpentry by the famous Mr Hicks of Dublin. He showed me a wonderful standard lamp made as an examination piece for Mr Hicks, in which three different types of wood were used, to great effect.

I admired some war medals which caught my eye and Peter informed me that an uncle of his had been killed in Belgium in 1916 during the Great War, and that these were his medals. He is also proud to have in his possession his uncle's periscope which was used in the trenches in those terrible days.

We proceeded to discuss our understanding of nature and the natural order of things. Peter feels that some farming methods nowadays go against the true cycle of nature, and that too many chemicals are used to the detriment of our health. We spoke of climate change, the destruction of the rain forests and unsound practices in the area of ecology.

Peter told me of a 15th century Spanish sailor who drew the exact topography of Antarctica before the icecap formed. NASA have since confirmed the veracity of the outlines on the original 15th century map. Peter's feeling is that we are now re-inventing things, and that much of what we are discovering had already been known in earlier ages. He spoke of early Celtic civilisations in Japan, of the fascinating clues to the past to be found in the Bible and the Koran, of the Druids, of the Indian culture of co-operation with nature, of natural cures, Dr Bach Remedies and water divining.

We had a long discussion on the merits and perhaps, the de-merits of poitin, and on the strength of the earlier porter supplied by the Guinness brewery. 'Triple X' got many a mention, as did the demand for malt for sick dogs. In fact, such was the demand that Peter, during his days at the Maltings, had eventually to harden his heart and refuse all requests. He did notice that all the sick dogs made a fine recovery nonetheless!

I listened with fascination to the story about Peter's uncle, Dr Watson, who was an intern at Sir Patrick Dunn's Hospital in Dublin. Eamon de Valera was in command at Boland's Mills during the Rising at Easter Week 1916, and he spoke to Dr Watson about the imminent surrender to the English. Dr Watson, thankfully, kept a detailed account of events taking place around the hospital on all the days of that eventful week until the surrender order was given.

I was shown some really wonderful old books, lovingly gathered by this dedicated bibliophile. A real gem was a *History of Ireland,* written in 1673 and annexed to it was a chronology for the years 1210-1350. From this Peter read an account of a great freeze in Dublin in 1338 when the Liffey was frozen over and fires were lit on the ice to boil herrings.

Two letters, written to Dr Watson in Dublin by Gordon of Khartoum in 1884, make fascinating reading, particularly one written on 26th November, just a few days before the writer's brutal murder.

As the evening began to draw in and I reluctantly considered taking my leave, I was told some interesting facts about the first hurling game to be recorded historically in Ireland, about the hurleys of olden times and the beauty, skill and elegance of the sport of hurling.

As I took my departure, I thanked the circumstances which had guided me to old Castle House on that October evening, and to my meeting with Peter Read, a man of great knowledge, intellect and charm.

Michael Collins, High Street, Newport, Co Tipperary

CD No. 9
Time: 50.18
Date Recorded: September 2005

In my journeys around the county of Tipperary over the past couple of years, several people suggested to me that I should meet with retired schoolteacher Michael Collins from Newport. One day in late September 2005 I arrived at Michael's home and sat down with him to record his recollections and memories of a long and fruitful life in the teaching profession.

Michael was born in Newport in 1937, attended the local convent and the Boys National School and later, for six years, he cycled to Limerick each day to attend CBS in Sexton Street. In 1956 he began his teacher training in St Patrick's College, Dromcondra, Dublin and his career began in Cahir in 1958. He was appointed Principal of Birdhill National School in 1960 and taught there till his early retirement in 1999.

Michael recalled that in the early days of his career, the children would bring a few sods of turf for the fire each day, and the dust floor had to be sprinkled with water and swept every evening after school. In 1965 a new school was built in Birdhill and this saw the end of the blackboard and easel, the inkwell and blotting paper.

The school Inspectors, Michael recalled, were a varied group of men, some were excellent individuals, others more difficult. There was huge pressure exerted on teachers in those days by the Inspectors, most of whom conversed only in Irish and Michael laughed as he said, "you wouldn't be the first to break into English."

The teaching of the Catholic religion was always very important in schools, as children were prepared for First Communion and Confirmation. In the early days, three local schools would be brought together at Confirmation time and the Bishop would examine the children on their catechism individually. As time went on, a Diocesan Inspector would come to the school, in place of the Bishop, and send in his report, based on the answers given by the children.

In Michael's early days at Birdhill, he taught 3rd, 4th, 5th and 6th classes. There was huge emphasis on Irish and maths, and penmanship was of the utmost importance. The subjects taught were Irish, English, Maths, History, Geography and Singing.

Michael has an abiding interest in local history and when, in the 1960s, the Department of Education wrote to all primary schools requesting that the old Inspectors' Report Books be sent to Dublin, presumably for burning, Michael disregarded the request, as he savoured the history held within the covers of the Report Books. He told me that there were amazing details of minor misdemeanours to be found within the books, for instance, clocks stopped, and a teacher's bicycle being kept in the classroom instead of in the yard!

The books describe a humorous event which occurred in the 1930s when it was decided to introduce nature study into the curriculum for primary schools. An inspector, whose real interest was in Irish and maths, asked the teacher to take a nature class. The teacher sliced an apple, held it up to the class and asked the colour of the inside of the apple. "White" came the answer from the class and the inspector immediately declared that the subject was exhausted, and that the important business of the day could now begin, with the examination of Irish and mathematics.

The names of the earlier teachers at Birdhill were recalled, as was a Parish Priest who was a wonderful support to schools in the locality.

Michael's interest in the GAA is all consuming, especially in the game of hurling, and he recalls the day when he was supervising the boys at a game of hurling in school, long after the lunch break had ended. This, of all days, was the day when the inspector decided to call! Along with a former pupil Michael has written a history of the GAA, and he told me that amazingly, a team never left Newport without a Ryan playing on it. We had a most interesting discussion on the Ryan family's deep roots in Tipperary up until the Cromwellian times. He has always taken great pleasure in research, and mentions the Civil Survey of 1654, which lists all the old landowners and the property they owned in land and houses. Many Ryans are mentioned in the Survey, and also some variations on the Ryan name.

It was lovely to listen as Michael listed the names of old townlands locally. He told me the name Birdhill means the hillock of the white bird, which name has its origins in an ancient legend involving Oisín and his exploits on his return from Tir na nÓg. When I spoke to Michael he was happily employed on the writing of a history of the local creameries and having taken the summer of 2005 off, he was greatly looking forward to returning to his research in the archives in Dublin. It was clear to me that here was a man who had taught the children of Tipperary for over 40 years and was now immersed in his research of local history for the pure joy and satisfaction to be gained from it.

It was a real pleasure for me to spend time with Michael Collins of Newport, teacher, scholar and gentleman.

The Late Sr Consilio O'Toole, Newport, Co Tipperary

CD No. 10
Time: 42.45
Date Recorded: February 2004

As I sat in the parlour of the Mercy Convent in Newport in February 2004, awaiting the arrival of Sr Consilio O'Toole, I reflected on her life of obedience and service which had spanned 64 years in the Mercy Order. Sr Consilio came to the Mercy Convent in Newport in 1950 and was to spend 48 years of her life in this fine old place.

Nora O'Toole first saw the light of day at Rear Cross, seven miles from Newport. Her parents were farmers and Nora was the eldest of six children. During her Leaving Cert year, one of the nuns at Doon suggested that the religious life may suit her. "I began to think a bit" said Sr Consilio to me now, as she recalled those earlier days and the major decision she faced. Once the decision was made, her family were very happy to receive the news and she entered the Convent of Mercy in Doon on 24th September 1940. Three weeks later, her father died, having been unwell for some time, and due to the strict regime enforced by the religious orders at that time, Sr Consilio was not allowed home to attend the funeral.

It is difficult to imagine today the reality of that strict regime, but she told me that she accepted unquestionably her inability to attend the funeral, as she had understood the rules when she entered the Mercy Order. Six years later, her sister was to die of leukaemia at the tragically early age of 22 years. Sr Consilio was allowed home to see her before she died, but once again could not attend the funeral.

On 1st July 1943, Sr Consilio was professed as a Sister of Mercy, and until 1945 trained as a primary teacher in Carysfort Training College in Dublin. She taught first class in Doon until 1947, and declared with a smile that she loved teaching and she loved the children. Her next teaching position was in Cappamore Primary School, where she enjoyed three happy years teaching the senior infants. In 1950 she was called upon to teach Secondary Top in Newport, which involved teaching the older children up to Inter Cert standard. St Consilio's pupils comprised the girls of the 1st and 2nd years.

All this discussion of education and teaching reminded Consilio of her own schooldays at Rear Cross National School. "You'd be laughed at for wearing shoes in hot weather" she said, as she remembered the barefoot run to school in the early summer months. After school, between Easter and May, there was turf to be footed in the bog, and during the summer months, hay to be saved.

The family was quite self-sufficient in those days and visited the shops only to buy flour, tea and sugar. As she grew up there was very little gallivanting allowed, though card games were common when neighbours would call to the house in the evenings. I chanced asking a most unsubtle question about any boyfriends in those days and Consilio laughed as she assured me that there had been none!

Emigration was part of life locally in the 1930s during the Economic War, when a great number of young people took the boats to England and America. Many girls left home to train as nurses in England and Consilio initially had an interest in nursing but her teaching career was to prove totally fulfilling.

Having taught primary school children for over 25 years, Sr Consilio left Tipperary to study for a Degree in Irish and English in Galway and later, in 1969, studied for a Higher Diploma in Education in Cork. She always had a deep love of history and taught the subject to Junior Cert level. The years of the Civil War were a time which held an abiding interest for her in her teaching of history. "You'd have to be very cagey teaching that" she told me, due to the fact that the years between were not many, and people's sensitivities had to be respected.

I was keen to find out where her loyalties lay in the matter of the politics of those days, and she said that her mother had canonised Michael Collins as she did herself, until she saw the Neil Jordan film *Michael Collins*. This had the effect of turning her against Collins somewhat due to the violence with which he was involved in those bitter days.

She still felt that Collins did his very best at the Treaty negotiations in London in 1921, and that De Valera had instructed the negotiators to get "peace at any cost", only later to refuse to accept the terms.

Sr Consilio witnessed immense change in the religious life during her sixty four years of ministry. She recalled the old black habit worn by all the sisters in the earlier days, with the long beads and the leather belt. In 1965 this changed, and "I was glad to be rid of it" she told me emphatically. In 1968 she made her first visit home in 28 years, apart from the brief visit to her very ill sister, and she was delighted with that taste of extra freedom, while having no regrets about the regulations of previous years.

I asked Sr Consilio which part of her religious life was the happiest, and she had no hesitation in replying that she prefered her life as it was then, when compared to the earlier days. She took each day as it came, and was always kept very busy. She still helped with the tuition of pupils in the Irish language if she was asked to do so, and very much enjoyed the work. While the language was not spoken in her own home, she recalled her father telling her that his father would regularly receive visits from a priest at Thurles College, during which they would spend hours conversing wholly in Irish.

She recalled an occasion shortly after her father's death, when the neighbours were helping her mother on the farm. They found goose eggs among the potatoes being dug. Her mother was very upset, knowing that the eggs were put there as part of the workings of a pisheog, designed to kill the crop. She immediately burnt the eggs which was known to kill the spell, and that year they had a better crop of potatoes than any of the neighbouring farms.

There was one place in the country where Sr Consilio always felt completely free and happy, and that place is Ballinskelligs, in Kerry, where the Superiors of the Order bought a holiday house in 1959. It was here she saw the sea again after many years, and as she described the experience of holidaymaking and swimming during the annual fortnight in Kerry, she smiled in contented and peaceful recollection.

I was very sad to hear some time later that Sr Consilio had gone to her eternal reward and I was very glad indeed that I had been given the opportunity to meet and to reminisce with such a spiritual and dedicated lady, who had spent her long and fruitful life in the service of others.

St Mary's Convent of Mercy, Newport in the early days

The late Roy Mooney, The Doon, Co Offaly

CD No. 11
Time: 50.36
Date Recorded: January 2004

In January 2004, I spent a most pleasant afternoon in an historic Georgian house at The Doon, Co Offaly where a wonderful log fire burnt in the hearth, and I was delighted to find myself in such pleasant company. My host was Roy Mooney, a most interesting and entertaining man, and I was to hear with much regret some months later, that Roy had passed away in his 91st year.

That January day I began by enquiring about the Mooney family of The Doon and was told that the lineage goes back to the Monarch of Leinster in 120 AD. The present house is built on the spot where the family have lived for over 600 years. The atmosphere of living history was very apparent to me and I enquired if anything of a supernatural nature had ever occurred within the walls of the house. Roy proceeded to tell me about something extraordinary experienced by his wife Kitty, on a memorable day in the 1960s.

The family were all away for the day, except for Kitty who had been feeling unwell, and was resting in bed. The door of the bedroom was open, and suddenly she became aware of a presence in the room. She looked towards the door and saw a man dressed in 17th century clothing which included a green livery coat. An ancestor of the Mooneys owned such a coat, which is still in the house and the family call him 'Bottle Green.' When Kitty saw the man at the door, she said "Oh, Bottle Green" whereupon he turned and disappeared. This happened in mid afternoon on a fine summer's day in full daylight, so he was not an imagined figure emerging from the shadows of an old house filled with dark corners.

Roy had some amazing stories to relate about the reign of the Black and Tans in the locality and about the Civil War. A military patrol of the Black and Tans would travel from Athlone to Birr and back each day, and they would fire at random into any sheltered area when they felt under threat from attack. At the age of 6 years, Roy remembered a ferocious knocking and banging on the front door of the house one night. The Black and Tans were digging themselves out of a trench cut across the road nearby and some of the soldiers had spread out across the lawn. They were firing indiscriminately and bullets were whizzing off the front of the house. A group of their comrades heard the firing and came to their aid but such was the confusion that some of the military were shot by their own forces.

During the Civil War men from both sides of the divide would come to the house and demand to be fed, and one night Roy had to give up his bed to some of their number. Local people felt sorry for the disruption to the family and sent a message to the house to say it was to be raided, so there was a swift exit and Roy was glad to reclaim his bed.

I enquired about ring forts in the vicinity and was told that there were eleven single ring forts locally and one triple ring fort on a nearby hill.

I heard a story about Robert Emmet, who is reputed to have called to the house while he was on the run. He was fed in the servants' hall and once rested and restored he left, having offered profuse thanks to the master.

Some interesting details emerged about the Shrine of St Monaghan, which is reputed to hold the bones of the local saint. In the 11th century the bones were disinterred and placed in a beautifully crafted shrine, and placed in Boher Church, which is three miles east of The Doon. The original thatched church caught fire on one occasion and the shrine was placed, for safe keeping, in the library at the Mooney house, where it remained for some years.

At this stage we were joined by Kitty Mooney, who comes originally from Galway city and whose surname before marriage was O'Dea. She explained that the shrine was in need of restoration in years gone by, and as it was to go to London for this purpose, it was opened and the bones removed. A medical man, who saw the bones, remarked that the leg bones were terribly distorted and as folklore had always maintained that Saint Monaghan was lame, this was taken as proof that the bones were indeed true relics.

We had a most interesting discussion on poitin, and about bottles hidden amongst sods of turf, about hurling and the making of the hurleys of old. I was shown an embroidered crest of the Metge family, a wonderful old travelling trunk used for transporting an army officer's silver to India, and a piece of polished limestone fashioned into a writing piece to hold a quill and incorporating a section for fine sand, used for blotting ink. This piece came from the nearby castle, the stronghold of the Mooneys, and is dated 1723.

As I left the house, the January afternoon made its presence felt as Roy Mooney opened the front door, and I was loath to step back into the cold light of the present having spent some very warm and happy hours surrounded by memories, artefacts and stories of the past.

Kitty Mooney, The Doon, Co Offaly

CD No. 12

Time: 74.03

Date Recorded: January 2004

My earlier visit, in January 2004 to the home of Roy and Kitty Mooney of The Doon, had been so interesting and enjoyable, I decided that I needed to hear more about this old Irish family and to see more of the fascinating historical artefacts and ephemera it had gathered over the generations. The blazing fire threw out its warmth to beat back the January chill, as I sat down with Kitty and Roy and prepared to listen.

The Mooney family came originally from areas around Roscommon and Monaghan, in fact the word 'Monaghan' is a distortion of 'Mooney'. Kitty remarked that the family was in The Doon "probably running around in goatskins" long before the ancient castle was built. The castle has been in a ruined state since 1790.

The present house was built in three different periods. Parts of the walls are six foot thick and run right down to the cellars. Beneath the room in which we sat run some interesting passageways and the servants quarters in the basement consist of nine rooms. Part of the house was built during the reign of George II. Roy told me that he had always felt that there may be a hidden passage within the six foot wall, and years ago he and another man knocked a hole in the wall, and did find a passage within in. Roy took a candle and gingerly stepped in through the hole, climbed up as far as he was able and came to a dead end. He feels that the passage may have been used as a hiding place in far off days.

I learned a great deal about a Mooney ancestor who was a most influential and powerful man during his lifetime. His name was Francis Edward Mooney and he was High Sheriff in the early 1800s. A beautiful miniature painting of Francis Mooney, in which he wears a green high-collared jacket and a periwig, hangs on a wall in the house at Doon and Roy and Kitty's family have christened him 'Bottle Green'.

About 40 years ago, Roy was examining a military typewriting box which had always been in the house, when he noticed two brass catches on the sides. On pressing these a secret drawer emerged, which held various pieces of paper. One was a £1 note, drawn on the Provincial Bank, Athlone, and had been hidden there since the days of 'Bottle Green'.

Again, during the 1960s, Roy decided to examine the contents of an old desk, which had lain undisturbed for as long as he could remember. He was thrilled to stumble upon his great great grandfather 'Bottle Green's' books, which enumerated fascinating details about the life and times of this most impressive individual who died in 1842. He kept meticulous records of his staff, their wages, his household and farm income and expenses. Kitty quotes from one book, "today, by the grace of God, I engaged John Hopkins. I am to pay him 12 guineas Irish per year." On another occasion he wrote, "I gave John Hopkins 2 shillings to bury his mother, 6d for boards for coffin." He later noted that he had to sack John Hopkins, being unhappy with the company he kept!

Also in the desk Roy found a Famine Book. A soup kitchen operated from the house in those terrible days in the 1840s and careful accounts were kept of the amount of rice and yellow meal which arrived from Birr to feed so many souls. The huge cauldron which was used to cook the food for the starving people may still be seen in the yard of the house.

In the early 1800s a shrine containing a relic consisting of bones of St Monaghan was brought to the house for safe keeping, as the church in which it was housed had been damaged by fire. It was kept in the library for several years, and around the feast day of the Saint, crowds of local people would arrive, knock on the door, and make their way upstairs to venerate the shrine. Local people who had fallen out would also come once their differences had been resolved, to shake hands and stamp their feet, and swear an oath of friendship.

The children of the house would also venerate the shrine in their own juvenile way, by sticking chicken bones through the decorative openings in the shrine These were discovered, to some mild surprise, in the 1930s when the Saint's bones were being removed from the shrine, as it was to be sent to London for restoration. Roy and Kitty feel that as the house was used in earlier days to provide shelter and protection for the shrine, any ideas of burning the dwelling in the 1920 may have been discounted.

I heard some dramatic and frightening stories of events at the house during the reign the Black and Tans and later during the Civil War. Roy's father was accused of being "King of the Sinn Feíners" by a less than sober Captain in the Black and Tans, who was interested in the whereabouts of a cave on the lands where he felt ammunition may have been stored. As he and his men would have to cross dangerous terrain, including woodlands, to access the cave he felt disinclined to undertake the search and requested Roy's father to do it in his stead – a request which was politely but firmly refused.

The Mooney home is a treasure trove of history and before I left, Kitty read from some letters dating from the 1700s and 1800s, written to members of the family. These letters are in themselves little portals to our past in all its richness, variety and colour.

Reluctantly I left Roy and Kitty Mooney that January evening in 2004, pleased with the realisation that I had somehow helped to capture the essence and warmth of the family and its long and honourable history.

A short time later I was to hear of the death of Roy Mooney of the Doon, in his 91st year and I mourned the passing of a fine gentleman, whom I feel privileged to have known and recorded.

Miniature silhouette of "Bottle Green"

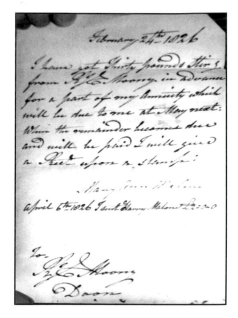

Receipt to Francis Edward Mooney.
February 24th 1826.

George Cunningham, Roscrea, Co Tipperary

CD No. 13
Time: 51.32
Date Recorded: May 2005

Since I began my travels through Tipperary collecting the rich oral tradition of the county, I have on several occasions encountered the name 'Monaincha'. When I first heard it described as "The Holy Island of Monaincha" I was gripped by curiosity and I made my way to Roscrea to talk to my friend George Cunningham, teacher, author and historian, and a man steeped in the history and lore of his native place.

My curiosity was somewhat sated one May afternoon in 2005, at George's house in Parkmore, Roscrea. The house is a treasure trove of books and manuscripts which I was sorely tempted to examine, but we had a mission on that day; to see the ruined monastery and discuss the origins of the Holy Island of Monaincha.

As we left Parkmore to begin our journey, George told me that Monaincha was one of his favourite places – a hidden treasure known as the 31st Wonder of the World, which could be described as the 'Sceilig of Inland Ireland'. The monastery was built on a bog island, originally known as Inis Locha Cre, and was first recorded as a retreat of local saints Cronán, Molua and Canice.

We paused on our journey in the heart of the heritage town of Roscrea to view the site of Cronán's settlement, the remains of which can be seen on either side of the present road. There has always been a road here, even in ancient times, and this was one of the reasons why the monastery was built at Monaincha.

During the 9th century, the monastery reflected the wealth of the church, as can be deduced from viewing the Roscrea Broach, which is second only to the Tara Broach, and which proclaims the wealth of its designers and producers. After the Reform Movement, some of the monks had become dissatisfied with the way life was lived in Roscrea. They retreated to Monaincha in about 800 AD lead by Hilary, Anchorite and Scribe, taking only, it is said, "the brown bread of Roscrea".

As we journeyed on, we passed by Birchgrove House, the home of the local landlords, who, in the late 18th century, founded the distillery which produced the famous Roscrea Whiskey, which is well documented in the literature of the 1800s and acclaimed for its taste, beauty and popularity.

I felt we had travelled back in time, once we abandoned the car and set foot on the bog road which leads to the islands and which up until 200 years ago, had been submerged beneath the lake. There are two islands here, Ladies Island and the Men's Island. In the late 12th century Geraldus, the Anglo Norman chronicler, recorded this site as Insula Viventium, the island on which no one could die. In the Middle Ages, the site was known as Inis na mBeo. George feels that this referred to the practice of pilgrims arriving here to have their sins wiped out, who could die peacefully only when this was accomplished. Geraldus was not above jazzing up the story for his colleagues at Oxford, and thus the site became known as the 31st Wonder of the World.

George recounted for me the four famous Irish sites of pilgrimage in ancient times: Croagh Patrick in Connaught, Glendalough in Leinster, St Patrick's Purgatory in Ulster and Monaincha in Munster, as recorded in the life of St. Kevin.

In the 1790s the lake was drained, the church site on the main island was walled by the Birch family and public burials there were halted. We stood in front of the ruined church, with its glorious Romanesque doorway, and could only gaze in awe at the craftsmanship involved and wonder at the skill, strength and ingenuity required to transport the stone to this isolated spot.

George described in loving detail the 12th century High Cross with its clothed figure of Christ, and its earlier base which incorporates biblical scenes, and could date from the 9th or 10th century.

We walked through the doorway and stood in the nave as George related to me the story of Cromwell's demand to be told the way to Monaincha from Roscrea, and of the terrified woman who was disturbed at her baking by his troops and the dastardly consequences of this sequence of events.

We moved on to the sacristy, which is a later addition to the main building. It is thought that this was built in the 15th or 16th century, as deduced from traces of the imprint of wickerwork on the plaster. We climbed the steps to the upper level of the sacristy and I stood and gazed at the late autumn landscape in all its colour and variety. We sat by the window, and George described for me some fascinating pilgrims and pilgrimages this place had seen over the centuries. He recalled a visit made by more modern pilgrims who were led by the late Archbishop of Dublin, George Otto Simms, when prayers were said in Latin, Greek agus as Gaeilge.

George himself became interested in this place in the 1960s, when as a teacher in Roscrea, he suggested to the parish priest that the pilgrimage could be revived. In August 1974, as a result of this suggestion, about 2,000 people from the parish of Roscrea walked to the Holy Island, where Mass was said. This is a memory very dear to George Cunningham, and to many local people who participated in the pilgrimage on that August day.

We sat for a while and reflected on the factors which make this ancient site of retreat and pilgrimage so unique and influential. There is a vibrant sense of holiness and goodness here, along with a deep feeling of ageless beauty and peace, and I was very pleased to hear that the office of Public Works are a wonderful support to the local people in their efforts to cherish and preserve their own unique heritage. The deeply spiritual feeling for this ancient place was so evident in George Cunningham's narrative, that I suggested we collaborate in the production of an aural guide to this holy site. The resulting CD, entitled *The Holy Island of Monaincha, Roscrea, Co Tipperary* is now on general release.

As we left the Holy Island and walked back along the causeway, I looked back at this ancient place of prayer and vowed to return again one day to sit in silence and reflect on a world where holy men lived out their lives of work and peace at Inis na mBeo, the Holy Island of Monaincha.

The Holy Island of Monaincha

Hannah and Violet Cahill, Clonderrig, Co Offaly

CD No. 14
Time: 57.58
Date Recorded: January 2004

On a raw January afternoon in 2004 I knocked on the door of the Cahill home at Clonderrig and was welcomed into the warmth of the kitchen by Hannah and Violet Cahill.

Both sisters are in their 80s and are a wonderful advertisement for country living and hard work in the outdoors. They have always lent their hands to any work which was necessary on their 80 acre farm, and have a great recollection of the joys of ploughing with a pair of horses in days gone by.

Both ladies conclude that their schooldays were very happy ones and though they came from the only Protestant family attending the local school, they were never made to feel that they were any different to the other children. In later years, a contemporary of theirs told them that as children at school, they had never known that the Cahills were non Catholic.

Hannah recalled that their house was always popular with local children in those days, who would come to play and enjoy the animals on the farm. I asked Hannah to describe her memories of the killing of the pig, and the dressing and salting, as my eye was caught by the old meat hooks in the ceiling, a real reminder of other days.

Hannah and Violet's father was one of eight brothers, seven of whom, including himself, served in the R.I.C. He retired from the force before marrying a Miss Griffith from near Clara, who at 28 years of age was somewhat younger than her husband. The couple met at Clara at a meeting house, were to lead a happy married life, and Mrs Cahill lived in Clonderrig until she died in her 93rd year.

We discussed the crops grown in former days, the buttermaking in the dairy, and I heard that when the girls were small their mother would rise at 5 a.m. in summer to churn the butter in the cooler hours before the sun rose in the sky.

There was talk of poultry, and hens hatching at the bottom of dressers, and of a neighbour who happily worked around the kitchen with a sow and her little bonhams lying nearby on a bed of straw.

The sisters recalled their late brother who worked with them on the farm until his death. As a child he spent all his spare time making model planes and was not too keen on school, though he was a beautiful writer whose handwriting copies were always praised highly by his teachers.

Hannah told me that she emigrated to Australia for two years between 1952 and 1954. It took six weeks of travelling from England to Australia, and on arrival she worked with a family, caring for the children. Prior to this she had known nothing about the country and had seen Australia only as a place on a map. She also spent some time in Cornwall working at a hotel, but was happy to return home to Clonderrig and her family.

Not without a certain trepidation, I enquired of the ladies if there had ever been any significant men in their lives. They laughed heartily, and Hannah declared that "you would need great qualifications for marriage" and with Violet's urging she proclaimed that one would need "the love of Christ, the patience of Job, the wisdom of Solomon and the strength of Samson." Once the laughter had died down, Hannah suggested that we take a look at the yard outside, so we donned our coats and ventured forth.

There were some lovely old stone buildings to be seen and a fine bank of turf was stored in one of them. Hannah told me that she had always saved the turf herself until the previous year. We had a look inside the barn which had been used to store corn, and here we were greeting sleepily by Tom and Brownie, two of the little cats which inhabit the farmyard. Inside the barn, in the dim light, shone two lonely old pieces of country furniture, a press and a flour bin, painted in bright colours as all kitchen furniture used to be.

The January cold began to bite, so we made our way back to the warmth of the kitchen and over a cup of tea Hannah and Violet demonstrated for me the various noises they would make to call the animals in the old days. Some animals were called by name, including Ned the donkey, though it was recalled that a certain visiting clergyman would always address the same donkey by the name of his bishop!

I was so pleased to have met with Hannah and Violet Cahill at their fine old house, and to have listened to some great recollections of hard work, industry and fun. I took my leave of them that evening with a better understanding of Christian lives lived to the fullest in gentleness and in peace.

Jim Tiernan, Monroe and Islandmore, Lough Derg

CD No. 15
Time: 48.40
Date Recorded: September 2005

While collecting oral material around the Portroe area of Tipperary in September 2005, I stopped for a chat with a gentleman who was busily and happily working in his garden. I introduced myself to Jim Tiernan who very kindly invited me into his home to talk and to reminisce about other days.

Jim was born in England and in 1939, on the outbreak of war, he and his brother and sister arrived home to Ireland with their mother. His father was a tradesman who was not allowed home until the war ended and in 1945 he bought 30 acres of land on Islandmore in Lough Derg, and built a house for his family there.

Jim's grandfather had come from Athlone to live on the island in the mid 1800s, caretaking a house for the O'Meara family. He was an eel fisherman by trade, who would bring his catch from the island to Nenagh from whence it was transported by train to Dublin and on to Billingsgate in London. He married a lady named Minnie Ryan from Garykennedy and they reared a family of ten children.

Jim recalled a tragic occasion when his grandfather's brother and two men named Cleary were coming back to the island from the mainland. Their boat capsized in rough weather and all three men were lost.

When Jim was 13 years old, he became unwell and spent four and a half years in various hospitals. He later lived for some time in England before returning to live in Monroe in 1973. His house had previously been owned by the local blacksmith, Patrick Seymour, and the entrance gate to the property stands as a proud testament to Patrick's skill. The gate still stands sound more than 100 years after it was fashioned.

I was very keen to hear Jim Tiernan's recollections of island life in his childhood days, and the picture he painted for me was one of great happiness and great hardship. He recalled getting up in the early mornings for school, being rowed across to the mainland by his father, Michael, and then walking two and a half miles to school. I could hear in his voice the shivering young boy who placed cardboard across the frosty seat in the boat on many a winter's dark morning. His father would collect his three children from the mainland after school and row them home, but once or twice, due to severe weather, he was unable to make the journey and the children were then kept for the night in their uncle's house on the mainland.

Life on the island moved at a slow and peaceful pace, and the only real outings the family enjoyed were the trips to Mass in Whitegate, on Sunday mornings. A kindly local garda would overlook the adults' regular weekly bottle or two of Guinness in the pub in Whitegate after Mass, which were partaken with pure pleasure outside of opening hours. There was always one other call to be made after Mass for nourishment for the journey back to the island. The Hayes family of Whitegate are remembered with gratitude for the wonderful breakfasts they provided for the islanders on many a Sunday morning.

I enquired of Jim if any archaeological remains were evident on the island in his youth, and he remembered the ruins of a church and some ancient stones bearing weather-beaten images of crosses. There is a story told locally about the monks who inhabited the island since before Cromwell's time, and who, while retreating before the Cromwellian troops, threw the church plate and chalices into the lake, so that they would not fall into the persecutor's hands.

After a short search in his house, Jim found some old photographs of his family, and one in particular was fascinating due to the history it showed. Jim's grandparents and eight of their ten children, stand outside their house on Islandmore. Jim calculated that the image was taken in 1894, when his father, Michael, was about 10 years of age. An English doctor came to the island at that time to fish, and as he was a camera enthusiast, he asked the family to pose for him one May morning, and a charming record now exists of an island family long since gone to its eternal reward.

The Shannon river froze over in the winter of 1963, and another photograph shows Jim and his uncle pushing a boat across one mile of ice to get to Puckane for supplies for the family on the island, which was icebound for seven weeks at that time. A journalist named Joe Keane, who worked with the *Farmers Journal* met them in Puckane and listened with fascination to their adventures of the morning. He recorded them there and then, and took the historic photograph.

Jim's father decided, during that long winter that the time had come to leave his island home, where every field had a placename, where at Christmas he would place a huge trunk of a tree behind the open hearth to keep his family warm for months, where he would fish for eels, pike, perch and trout and would salt them in barrels for the bleak winter months, where he raised his family in safety and in peace.

Jim showed me a list his father had written in beautiful copperplate, of prices of goods on the market in 1944, some of which were:

> 15 year old horse £14-15-0
> 7 year old mare £27-0-0
> 2 gallons petrol £0-6-8
> 6 lbs turnip seed £1-0-0

His father had also kept a record of the old placenames used on the island and when Jim suggested I call another day to see this and some other interesting items, I was more than happy to agree. I left Monroe that evening already looking ahead eagerly to my return visit to this most gracious and interesting gentleman of Islandmore in Lough Derg.

View of Lough Derg

The late Jim Tiernan Snr and Jim Tiernan Jnr pushing their boat on the frozen lake in 1963.

CD No. 16
Time: 67.51
Date Recorded: September 2005

Only a week had passed since my first visit to Jim Tiernan's home as I made my way once again to visit him, to sit by his fireside to recall his early days, and to discuss how life was lived on Islandmore on Lough Derg by his parents and grandparents in former days.

As I settled myself beside the fire that fine September evening, Jim remarked that in the old days on the island they would often be without paraffin oil for the lamps, so would spend the long night with only the flickering light of the fire.

Life was hard then and there was little comfort to be had. Jim recalled in detail, the onset of an illness which struck him in February 1947, when he was 13 years old and working with his father, getting sugar beet to the shore to be loaded on the boat for the mainland. He began to feel very unwell, went home to bed, and the following day was unable to stand, due to the pain in his leg. The doctor was summoned, but as he was snowbound, five days were to elapse before he reached his patient, whom he diagnosed with tuberculosis. The following day, Jim's father and uncle brought the boy to the mainland. He was taken to Ennis hospital where he was to be without visitors from home for seven long weeks, as the lake was frozen over and his parents were unable to leave the island.

He was to pass four birthdays and three Christmases in various orthopaedic hospitals and has great memories of being entertained by the stars of the Gate Theatre while in hospital in Dublin one Christmas. Jimmy O'Dea, Maureen Potter, Rose Brennan and tenor Arthur Cox are remembered with great gratitude, almost 60 years later.

Our thoughts drifted back to the island as I enquired about the wildlife in evidence there in former days. Foxes were never seen, but there was no shortage of rabbits and otters. Rats were a great nuisance to the islanders and Jim maintains that they would swim across from the mainland on scavenging expeditions.

He recalled setting traps for ducks by the shoreline in winter when food was scarce. One of the O'Meara family owned a gun, but the licence covered only the shooting of vermin and did not allow the shooting of game for the pot.

Jim began to recall the names of the islands close to his home at Islandmore, and a lovely lyrical litany they made. He spoke of Holy Island, and the burial ground there. I was told that Jim's father, Michael, recalled that once when the little field behind his father's house was being ploughed, human bones were unearthed, which had lain buried since the time of a battle fought with the Cromwellian forces. A priest was called to the island, and it was decided to rebury the bones and leave the place in peace. I enquired of Jim if the field had a name, and this prompted him to play a recording of his father's voice, made in the 1960s in which he recites the names of many of the island fields, and when he omits a few, Jim supplies them for me.

In the recording Michael Tiernan continues to detail events in his own father's time on the island, the number of houses inhabited or in ruins, the school which occupied one room in his house attended by 12 pupils at one time. Later the number of pupils was reduced to three before the school was eventually closed.

Michael also describes a trip attempted by himself and his brother to the mainland in 1963. The waters of the Shannon were frozen and fifty yards from shore, the ice cracked and they began to sink. The trip was swiftly abandoned. That night saw another severe frost, and in the morning they accomplished their mission and brought provisions back to their isolated and icebound home.

Another voice on the recording from the 1960s was that of Jim Tiernan's aunt Lizzie, who spoke of her schooldays and of Christmas on the island. Her parents would row across to the mainland and travel on to Nenagh to do the annual Christmas shopping. The house would be decked out with holly and ivy and a goose would be hung in front of a fine fire and basted continually with the fat which dripped into a pan. The bird took 3 to 4 hours to cook and was wonderful to taste. Jim recalled one Christmas as a child in his grandmother's house on the island. She was a marvellous cook and for Christmas she would grate some potatoes and soak them in water overnight. In the morning the potatoes were dried off and mixed with flour, herbs, salt and pepper and were baked slowly in a metal pot, placed on the fire with hot coals piled on the cover. Rabbits would also be cooked and the rabbit stock used for the very best vegetable soup, to warm the heart and soul on a December evening.

The hunger was creeping up on us both as we considered these Christmas feasts, so we partook of some tea as Jim continued to recall the parties held in the two houses on the island each Christmas night and on New Year's Eve.

Before I left, I asked him to relate to me a humorous story, involving a statue which was in need of a cleaning and how the job was undertaken by Jim during his time working at a hospital some years ago. I was prompted to enquire about this by a neighbour who felt that this was something that needed telling, and so it proved it be!

The bright September day was drawing to a close when I took my leave, and once again I promised that I would return to hear some more of the old recording of the voices of Michael and Lizzie Tiernan and further details of their long and fruitful lives lived in hardship and in happiness on Islandmore.

The Tiernan Family Islandmore c. 1894.

CD No. 17
Time: 11.37
Date Recorded: 1960s

As I sat beside the blazing fire in Jim Tiernan's house in Munroe in September 2005 I was transported back to the hard days of the early 1900s on Islandmore in Lough Derg. I listened, entranced, to a recording made during the 1960s with Jim's father, the late Michael Tiernan. He describes several remarkable incidents which occurred on the island of Islandmore during his lifetime and in earlier days.

In a clear, strong voice, he tells us that the area of the island covered 140 Irish acres, on which stood the ruins of a church and a graveyard. During the Cromwellian invasion, refugees came onto the island seeking sanctuary, the forces followed, and many people were slaughtered in the ensuing battle. The battle site was a field named Gortnasilla, which lay directly behind the house occupied by Michael's family in later years. As a child he recalls the time a local man began to plough the field, which had not been touched for generations. After a few minutes, he stopped the horses to check on the ploughed patch and discovered what he thought were human bones lying in the upturned soil. He tied his horses to a tree and went to get the owner of the field, and Michael's father, to check on his discovery. It was decided that a priest should be called, so two men rowed to Whitegate to get the parish priest, who came to the island and alerted the authorities in Dublin. Eventually the presence of human bones was confirmed and the decision was made to turn back the earth and to leave the field as it had lain for so many years, undisturbed and in peace.

Recalling that event in his young life reminded Michael of the many names of the fields on the island, and he listed them off without hesitation. There was Fairy Hill, Well Field, Church Field, Top of the Hill and many more. With a fine guffaw he named Still House Field and asked his audience to guess where it had got its name. The ruins of the house were still visible in the field when the recording was made in the 1960s.

When Michael's father, who came from Lough Ree beyond Athlone, first arrived on Islandmore in the mid 1880s, the ruins of 15 houses stood there. Each of the occupants would have owned a small-holding, barely living at subsistence level, and eventually, when Michael's parents married and moved to live at Islandmore, only three families remained, named O'Meara and O'Grady. Michael's father had made an agreement with Joe O'Meara to look after the stock on his holding and he thus have the house rent free. The Tiernan couple went on to rear six boys and four girls in that house.

Michael recalled a stirring tale relating to the visit of a midwife to the island to assist his pregnant mother one dark winter's night. At about 2.00 a.m. it became evident that medical assistance would be required for Mrs Tiernan, so two men rowed to Garrykennedy to collect the midwife. On arrival at her house they discovered that she was already assisting another mother, so they waited till she arrived home at about 4.00 a.m. When she heard that a trip to the island was imminent she declared, "I'll have to have a drop of 'medicine' first" and when Mr Tiernan assured her that they had 'medicine' on the island, she told him that she would need some for the journey across the lake "to limber me up." Ever afterwards she was known on the island as 'Limber', and many a mother was grateful to her and her 'medicine'.

The island school, which was attached to the Tiernan home, was built in 1900. Michael was born in 1905 and as the school had closed due to lack of pupils, he had to finish his schooling on the mainland, rowing two miles across the lake each morning before walking two miles to Kilbarron School. From the age of 10, he would row the boat also containing his brother and sister across the lake each day, if the weather was fine.

Michael Tiernan recalled the Shannon River being frozen on three occasions, the last of these being in the year 1963, when the island was cut off for seven weeks. Getting to the mainland became an absolute necessity on one occasion, as there was only enough flour among the three families on the island to make one small loaf. He describes in vivid detail the journey he made across the ice with his brother in their stockinged feet, pushing a boat, containing two bicycles for the onward journey to the shop at Puckane.

Though the recording was short in duration, it created a vibrant image of life lived in the teeth of winter's grip, of history unearthed, of youth, vigour and hard work and of gentle humour employed as a merciful salve upon the great hardship and isolation of island life.

Kathleen Hogan, Ballybrood, Caherconlish, Co Limerick

CD No. 18
Time: 52.47
Date Recorded: March 2004

On my travels around Ireland collecting the lore of the various counties, I have been very fortunate in meeting people who are interested in my work, and who have helped by introducing me to men and women in their localities who have wonderful stories to tell.

In March 2004, Breda Cleary from Limerick brought me to the home of Kathleen Hogan at Ballybrood and I am very glad that she did. Kathleen is a lady who has clear recollections of her childhood and early adult life, and recalls these far off days with a fine sense of humour and fun.

Kathleen's maiden name was O'Rourke and she was born in Kilcorman, Co Limerick, the youngest in a family of five boys and two girls. At the age of 17 years she began to attend dances at the local library, and on one memorable night General Eoin O'Duffy, the leader of the Blueshirts, arrived with some of his men. He asked Kathleen to dance. As they waltzed across the floor, he enquired of her if she had joined the Blueshirts and she thought it opportune to reply that she had, though it had never crossed her mind to do so! "T'would take you" said her friends, laughing, when she recounted this exchange later in the night.

As Kathleen was growing up, the family was very involved with the local gymkhanas and the foxhounds. The Harriers Club would meet every Wednesday and Saturday. There was no work done on the farm on those days, declared Kathleen, "only milk the cows in the morning and off then." The Harriers Club would organise dances in the locality, and on many a night, at least ten of Kathleen's friends and family would set out together on bicycles to Adare or Rathkeale to attend the dances. Kathleen shook with laughter as she recalled one evening of driving rain, when she took off on her bicycle with eight others to a dance in Adare. She had had a beautiful white dress made especially for the occasion, and put this, with a pair of silver slippers, into a bag in the carrier of the bicycle. On her arrival, she changed out of her sodden travelling clothes and dressed up in her new finery, only to discover that one of her little silver slippers had been exchanged at home by her brothers for a heavy hobnail boot. Recovering from her dismay she put on the boot and slipper and danced the night away, unperturbed if somewhat lopsided.

I asked Kathleen if she remembered the Black and Tan occupation of 1921, and she said that at nine years of age she remembered hanging onto her mother's apron with fear, during raids on their house. A cousin, who had joined the American Army and come home on leave dressed in his uniform, was asleep in bed in Kathleen's home one night when the Tans arrived. They pulled him from his bed, searched and questioned him closely, and hit him several times with the butts of their rifles.

She recalled another occasion at Ferry Bridge when the Tans drove at speed onto the bridge which had earlier been cut. Four of their number were killed. Reprisals were swift in coming and things were even worse as a consequence. The local men on the run would often stay at her house at night, where they would be fed. Afterwards they would sit up all night talking around the fire, fearful of falling asleep.

The Economic War was recalled when calves were being sold for 50 pence and Kathleen's family bought a white cow, an excellent milker, for £1. Rationing was in operation and on one occasion supplies were needed to feed the neighbours who were coming to help with the threshing. Kathleen was sent to Limerick one eventful day, to get tea and sugar from a cousin, who owned a bakery in the city. While there, she was introduced to her future husband and amid many a chuckle, she explained to me the sequence of events. In 1948 she and John Hogan married and settled at Ballybrood.

I was interested to know if she had came across any pisheogs or superstitions when she moved into her new home. She said that when she was newly married her husband warned her never to give out any eggs for hatching on a May weekend as it was considered unlucky. Also, on May Eve, Holy Water was taken to all four corners of the land which were then blessed. She also recalled having Mass said in the house on an occasion when a dead calf had been put into the water tank by persons unknown.

Laughter again overtook her as she recounted a story of going on strike during a family dispute, with her older brother, whilst living at home before she left to get married. While she had time on her hands during the strike she took up knitting, which she exchanged later for crochet work. She told me that she has made everything from a christening robe to a wedding dress and her exquisite work has travelled to many countries around the world, while it is treasured for its craftsmanship and its beauty.

Before I left I asked Kathleen to read for me her favourite prayer to St Brigid and as she held a St Brigid's Cross in her hands, she read the gentle words which began "A tiny cross made of rushes."

The light heart and laughter of Kathleen Hogan stayed with me as I travelled home to Kerry, and I vowed to visit her again to sit and listen to more of her memories of other happy days and to bask in the warmth of her humour and her sense of fun.

Margaret and Joe Rea, Cahir, Co Tipperary

CD No. 19
Time: 47.10
Date Recorded: May 2004

One afternoon, several years ago, while working at our antiques business in Tralee with my wife Jane, Joe and Margaret Rea, from Cahir, dropped in and before they left the premises an hour later, we had become firm friends and were looking forward already to our next meeting.

In May 2004, on a balmy afternoon, I drove up to the door of the Rea home which is set in a lush and flower filled garden, and surrounded on all sides by mature broadleaf trees. I was invited to sit in the garden with Joe, who told me that the house was built in 1770, is his ancestral home, and that he and Margaret have lived here for 36 years. Joe's father died when Joe was 14 years old, and from then onwards, he helped his mother run the farm. She came originally from Wexford and was a most progressive and successful farmer.

Joe was always an avid reader with a great thirst for knowledge, and once his schooling was finished, he attended an Adult Education course for 2 years, run by UCC in Clonmel, and graduated with a diploma in Economics, Social Science and Administration. He credits this period of study for his keen interest in economics and social science, which was to be sustained right through his years in public life.

He was elected President of Macra na Feirme in the 1960s, at a time when science was beginning to impact on farming. Joe reminded me that in the 1950s Ireland was importing butter from Denmark, and he remembers Jimmy O'Dea the comedian, at the time say "the Danes may have killed Brian Ború, but they won't kill me with their butter". In those days Ireland was producing enough food to be self-sufficient. As we spoke in 2004, however, the country was exporting 90% of its milk and cattle, 70% of its sheep and 50% of its pigs – in fact Irish farmers were producing enough food to feed 30 million people – a staggering contrast to the state of affairs which prevailed 50 years ago.

With a chuckle, Joe told me a story about a visit by Elizabeth Taylor to the Shelbourne Hotel in Dublin, which serves to illustrate the fact that surplus supply can be a major problem. The moral of the story was "a small amount of surplus can destroy the total product" and a bath full of champagne featured strongly in the story!

Joe Rea was elected President of the Irish Farmers Association in the 1980s, and he had many thought provoking and fascinating things to say regarding efficiency in farming, technology and agri-business, manufacturers, the marketing of farm produce, organic farming and niche markets. He was a great admirer of the late Pope John XXIII for his far sighted policies, and while Joe told me that he is not religious in a formal sense, he believes in the existence of God, and in society's great need of an anchor.

We sat at our ease and spoke about the wondrous landscape which enveloped us. This, according to Joe, is one of the most fertile valleys in the world, overlooked by the Knockmealdown Mountains and the Vee Pass. Cromwell, on his rampage through Ireland in the 1600s, wintered in Youghal, Co Cork, then marched over the Vee Pass into Tipperary and looked down on the lush valley below. Cromwell had been a farmer in Herefordshire, and, turning to his generals on that day he declared "there's a land worth fighting for!"

Joe and Margaret Rea first met at a Macra na Feirme dance. Joe paid warm tribute to his wife who raised their family and looked after the farm while he was out 'saving the world', a reference to the voluntary work he undertook over many years. He invited me into the house where I was welcomed warmly by Margaret, who was born in Donohill, six miles from Tipperary town "Dan Breen country" she assured me. Homeliness and calm enveloped me in this fine old farming house which was lively and busy on that day, with people coming and going all the time. Special mention was made of the marvellous neighbours who are always there to help if needed and Joe was adamant in his view that rural people are magnificent in their friendliness and helpfulness, once I ventured to suggest that people felt more isolated today than heretofore.

As we ventured down the hallway towards the kitchen, built around its gleaming Aga, we passed some very interesting prints hanging on the walls. My eye was caught by a map of Ireland, drawn in 1850, showing the routes taken by the Bianconi Coaches, and Joe was delighted to say that he had found the map in a junk shop in Brussels.

A framed poster of Daniel O'Connell, printed to mark the 100th anniversary of his birth, hung alongside. As a complete contrast, hanging cheek by jowl with 'The Liberator' was Queen Victoria, and it was obvious from his chuckle that Joe derives a certain amount of quiet glee from this incongruity.

Leaving the warmth of the kitchen, I was privileged to be invited into Joe's own special room, to which, according to himself, he and all his clutter, have been banished by Margaret. Here I was shown a fascinating collection of cartoons, published by *The Farmers Journal,* featuring Joe at significant times in his public life. He talked about visits he made to India, New Zealand, Ethiopia and South Africa, and his admiration for Mahatma Gandhi and Nelson Mandela was very evident as he recalled those visits.

I ventured to enquire if he had a notion to write an autobiography, but Joe was quick to respond with a laugh, saying that a book would have to wait till he was gone, as much of what he had to say would prove too controversial for his readership.

He mused that at funerals he has often heard people discuss the deceased, and say "he was a nice divil, and did nobody any harm." This is an awful waste of a life, according to Joe Rea, who feels a person should do good as well as never doing harm. I have to agree with him, as it is obvious that his own life has been dedicated to doing good for the farmers of Ireland, for their families and for the wider community.

The late Nora Humphreys, Newport, Co Tipperary

CD No. 20
Time: 77.10
Date Recorded: January 2004

In early January 2004, I was privileged to spend some hours in the company of a wonderful lady at her home in Newport, Co Tipperary. Nora Humphreys was full of life and laughter on that cold winter day and once she was satisfied that I was warm and comfortable, she began her life story, by recalling her parents and her early days at Clonbeg, outside Thurles. Her family, the Costellos, were farmers, and her mother had retired from teaching once her family came along. Nora was born in 1917 into a family of seven children, and in that busy household a very important person, named Nell Devaney, helped her mother with the rearing of the children. Nell had come to the family at 14 years of age, and was later to marry from the Costello home.

On her day off, Nell went to the races at Thurles on a day in June 1919, and, on her return to Clonbeg that evening she declared "that was the best day we ever had. Old Hunt was shot." Michael Hunt was District Inspector of British Police and was not a popular figure. That day in Thurles, he had been shot by two men, 'Big Jim' Stapleton and Sean Dunne. After the shooting, the men scaled a high wall, and crossed the Suir on three occasions before arriving at the Ryan Lacken home, and eventually at Killaloe. Sean Dunne, aged about 17, had been a boarder in Rockwell College and had left to join the Republicans, unknown to his parents. He was to spend 3 months in Killaloe recovering from pneumonia which he had contracted during that perilous journey.

Nora's mother and Nell Devaney would regularly provide food and lodging for the boys on the run in those days and would wash their clothes overnight and have them dried by the fire for the following morning.

As a child of three years old, Nora had a distinct memory from those days. One morning the postman came flying into the yard, threw his bicycle on the ground and ran into her house. She stood mesmerised in the yard as the back wheel of the bicycle kept spinning, and when she at last entered the kitchen her mother was putting hastily cut bread into the hands of two men who were wearing bandoliers and carrying rifles, and instructing them "get the holy water and go down." The Black and Tans were on their way, and the boys were heading down to Doyle's Valley, which had lush green banks on either side, providing good cover.

On another occasion, eight men were sleeping in the hay barn, and at daybreak one of them took the mirror off the kitchen wall, propped it up at the outdoor pump, and they all lined up to lather and shave. This image had remained stark in Nora's memory since the morning her three year old self had stood and watched and wondered.

She remembered, at this time being wakened at night by her uncle tapping on her aunt's bedroom door to alert her to the fact that he was taking the cross-cut, which was used to cut down trees, but not for firewood on that occasion.

During that terrible time her mother would tack up her black apron over the bedroom window at night, as she would need to light a candle to tend to her baby, and was fearful that the Black and Tans would shoot into the bedroom if they saw a light shining within.

Nora smiled as she recalled her schooldays at Clonbeg National School, where she began her education at four years of age. She remembered all the children in school bringing 2d each to buy an umbrella as a retirement gift for teacher Johnny O'Rourke. The date of his retirement was engraved on a silver band above the handle of the umbrella. Every Friday evening, the children paid 6d for dancing lessons which were conducted by Frank Kiely, originally from Ring, Co Waterford, who would accompany them on the tin whistle. She also recalled that in later years in Newport, every couple of months, a gentleman would come selling ballad sheets for 2d each. He would play 'The Rose of Tralee' on the melodeon and because he was not too physically robust, he was duly christened "the Pale Moon".

During the Second World War, her mother would sometimes go to Thurles to collect cigarettes, which were in very short supply. She had her own friendly suppliers in the town, and over the following weeks, she would dispense her supply to the smoking needy who would turn up at the house once the word of her bounty had spread.

As a child Nora clearly remembered being thrilled and frightened by the sight of a lock of golden hair, kept safely in a purse owned by Jack Hayes who worked on the Costello farm. Jack told his young audience that he had found the lock of hair on the banks of the river and that it had come from the head of the Banshee.

On May Eve, Nora's father would always cut a branch of whitethorn, and tie it upright to the railing on front of the house. The children would collect bunches of wild flowers and tie them to the branch of whitethorn. This was known as 'dressing the May bush' and was done in honour of the Blessed Lady.

She recounted for me the customs observed on Palm Sunday, Easter Sunday, St John's night, and on the Feast of St Martin, when a chicken's blood would be spilled at the two corners of the kitchen door. This was never washed off and remained until the rain came and cleaned it away. We spoke of the Pattern Day at St Patrick's Well on the 15th August, where the Rosary would be said all day long, and three sips of the water from the well would be drunk in honour of the Father, Son and Holy Ghost.

I was transported back to Clonbeg, to the year 1898 when Nora began to describe a wedding reception which had taken place in a specially cleaned and decorated hay barn. Nora's father had often recalled the scene; the February day with a scattering of snow on the ground, the tables brought by the neighbours which were covered with white sheets. Lined up along the tables were 15 brass candlesticks. Punch was made in jugs, from whiskey which had arrived in gallons, and the punch was poured from the jugs into pewter mugs. A local lady, who was a wonderful cook, had arrived the day before to attend to the catering, but on the big day she overindulged a little on the punch, and had a major mishap with the serving of a goose. Also the best man, who was taking a stroll in the snowy darkness, walked right into a dunghill and Nora's father had to rescue him and clean him off. The reception lasted till 6 a.m. the following morning when all and sundry had to head back, reluctantly, to the cold reality of the coming winter's day.

Nora had always loved to sing and I was treated to several of her favourite songs. 'The Blackbird' was a song she learned from a neighbour at Clonbeg. She described how to make candles using rushes which had been picked at a particular time of year, peeled and dried before being dipped into melted beeswax. She recalled Mick Ryan singing *The Foggy Dew* and *Kevin Barry* as he milked the cows at her home, and the fine music of the Billy Cummins Céilí Band from Roscrea. She sang for me 'The Three Flowers' which proudly recalled O'Dwyer, Emmet and Tone, and also a plaintive old verse of 'Galway Bay'.

Recollections of 'Neddy the Pluck' drew chuckles of glee from Nora as she recalled Neddy Hogan from Thurles, who would come to pluck 60-70 geese at the barn at Clonbeg. The children would watch him at work, and once the mound of feathers had reached a fine height, they would throw a kitten or a chicken over the half door onto the mound, and the world would come alive with feathers. 'Neddy the Pluck' who charged "tuppence a pluck" would jump up in a rage and call for their mother, who would have to remove the children and restore some semblance of peace before work could be resumed once again.

Nora's uncle, a priest home on holidays, leant on the half door of the barn one day as Neddy was at work, and asked him how he was, and Nora laughed heartily as she recalled his cheerful response – "wearing away like the end of a moon."

People such as Neddy coloured the countryside in those days and people such as the late Nora Humphreys are custodians of the old memories which are kept very much alive in story, song and laughter.

The late Nora Humphreys, Newport, Co Tipperary

CD No. 21
Time:
Date Recorded: January 2004

Before the bitter month of January 2004 had blown itself out, I made my way back to Newport to the home of Nora Humphreys, and once again prepared to be entertained royally by her stories, songs and fun.

My first question related to the compulsory tillage of the Emergency period during World War II, and Nora clearly remembered the 8 acres of potatoes sown at her old home at that time. The big potato digger "needed three horses under it", so her uncle would bring over his black mare to increase the horse power. The mare was a "sulky old rap" which would refuse to pull with the other horses, until Nora's father took control of the situation by giving her a rap with a stick to get her going.

At the meitheal, everybody would bring his own basket for the potato picking. A child and an adult would always be put to work together, because if the children were left to their own devices not a potato would see the bottom of a basket. The schoolmaster would be told in advance of the big day, just as he would be advised in May, when Mass was to be said in the house. The children were allowed time off school to attend the Mass, and Nora remembered clearly that her mother, early that morning, would leave tea, milk, bread, butter and sugar in the dairy for the children's breakfast, to be eaten after Mass before they left for school. The priest, the family and friends would all take breakfast in the parlour.

"Put off that radio. There's a match on Sunday" was Nora's father's constant command during summer days of long ago, when he feared for the life of the radio battery, as the weekend and the hurling match on the Sunday approached. He was a man who dearly loved music, and on a trip to town would give his daughter 1/6d to buy records, usually of céilí music, and the children would dance around the kitchen floor after tea in the evening.

Newport was one of the first places in the country to be electrified, so when Nora married and moved to Newport from Clonbeg, near Thurles in 1943, she was delighted to have electricity at her new home. In Clonbeg, candles and oil lamps had been the only source of light, and she recalled for me the double-wick oil lamp which hung from the centre of the ceiling, with a weight in the corner of the room to drop it down for cleaning and filling.

Nora Humphreys had great recall of events in the troubled times in Ireland during the years 1919-1922. Republicans Martin and Paddy Ryan Lacken were related to her by marriage and the connection was traced by Martin Kennedy who would come down from the mountains, sit by the fireside and begin "Norrie Moloney had seven daughters". He would list all the marriages of these girls, and "one married Ryan Lacken and one married Humphreys." The Ryan Lacken home was burnt by the Black and Tans, and Mrs Ryan Lacken and her 14 year old daughter Norrie, were lucky to escape with their lives. Matt Lacken, the head of the household, was held hostage in Newport Barracks at the time, and his two sons were on the run.

"The Civil War was very nasty. It was brother against brother" and a terrible time for families who split and fought against one another.

In later years, the Blueshirts would run dances around the locality, and dressmakers were kept busy making blue blouses for the women. Paddy Kinnane of Upperchurch, "a real gentleman and great Republican" would come to the concerts and "pull the socks up over the mouth of the pants and dance *The Blackbird* like a cork on the floor". This great image brought on the urge to sing, and Nora now put back her head, and relaxed into singing the lovely old tune *Dear Old Newport Town*.

Here by the Mulkear banks I sit
Mid the lovely flowers of June
The birds are singing cheerily
And the meadows in full bloom,
When on my boyhood days I think
The tears come rolling down
For in the morning I must leave
My dear old Newport town.

How lovely is the pigeon's coo
And sad the blackbird's lay.
And loud and high the thrush's song
On a long bright summers day
But I'll sit down and cry my fill
As the flood comes rushing down
And dashes through the Ivy Bridge
In dear old Newport town.

Adieu, adieu sweet Newport town,
Once more I'll say adieu
For many's the pleasant day I've spent
With comrades loyal and true
And if God spares me I'll return
To where the Mulkear waters flow
And when I die my bones will lie
In dear old Ballymackeogh.

Nora smiled as she told me that the sweet old song had been composed long ago by Mick Burke, the only son of a wealthy Newport businessman. Mick Burke and Jimmy Coleman would always follow the wren on St Stephen's night making sweet music, Mick with his melodeon, and Jimmy battering the floor in his hobnailed boots. They would collect money for porter for the dance to be held later on in the night at McGrath's house which was famous for its fine flag floor. "If ye bring me a few bottles of porter, ye can dance all night" McGrath would barter, and dance they all did, till somebody peeped through the shutters in the early morning to check if daylight had come. "Oh Lord, we were cracked" laughed Nora, in an ecstasy of happy recollection.

It is a well known fact that Tipperary is a hurling county of renown and I wondered if Nora and her sisters had ever played the national game. They played marbles and skittles, she informed me, but no camogie, though they'd hurl with the boys in their own fields. The boys were always looking for nice ashplants for making into hurleys and "would travel miles for it." After darkness had fallen, two or three of them would furtively cut the tree, and carry it home. It would then be cut into strips on wet days when no work on the farm could be done. Glass would be used to smooth off the hurleys, which were then bound with hoops. "My father knew every hurler from one end of the county to the other, and they'd all call in below. Bill Devaney would call, and give half the day talking about hurling".

We reluctantly left the glorious hurling fields of the memory and brought Nora back to the farm of her youth, and its customs. She described the crusheen, a short handled implement used at the well to wash potatoes. The basket of potatoes was put into the water and the potatoes were pounded with the crusheen till they were clean. She recalled, with obvious love, a neighbour of her early youth, who would rail against her husband for failing to return from the fair with the other men. "I'll give that fellow a good lambasting. I have 40 fires burnt waiting for him. He's a right old folamer" – a word used to describe a man who was never in a hurry home if there was a pub to be found on his way.

The same beloved neighbour, whose name was Jo, was wont to have some fun at the expense of Mick Ryan who would arrive for work on the farm on Monday mornings, still in his good clothes since Sunday night's dance. To torment and tease him she'd sing, "Youth and folly makes young men marry, and makes them sorry another day", all the while milking away industriously.

Nora and her siblings had their own individual jobs to do on the farm after school, and during the summer holidays. A job they loved was picking potatoes, because in between the picking they could practice their dance steps in their bare feet. "The ground would be battered flat from the jigging and dancing." Nora began to hum the tune of *Miss McClouds Reel,* and then broke into Irish as she counted out the steps the small bare feet battered into the clay.

"Haon, dó, trí, ceathar, cuíg, sé, seacht, and a hoan, dó, trí and a ceathar cúig, sé. Haon, dó, trí, ceathar, cuíg, sé, seacht, and a hoan, dó, trí, and a ceathar, cúig, sé."

It came as no surprise to me to learn, having grasped the essence of fun in the life of Nora Humphreys, that three nights before her wedding she was off up the hill with her brothers 'lamping' rabbits. Their father's greyhound, 'Blind John' accompanied them on their quest. Nora's brother had a car battery attached to his back, and a lamp to dazzle the prey, and in the excitement of attempting to catch a rabbit, 'Blind John' ran between Nora's legs and she ended up flat on her back on a sharp rock. Some days later, her lovely wedding outfit hid a bruised and blackened back, which had to be suffered in silence as her night-time lamping adventures were conducted in secret unknown to her innocent parents.

After her marriage, at her home in Newport, she would be up early in the mornings to light the fire and was sometimes visited by Dinny Galligan, who would sleep in the haybarn. In the mornings he'd be given a cup of tea, and would sit and smoke a cigarette by the fire, before leaving for his day's work on a neighbouring farm. One morning, Nora enquired if there had been any news in Newport the previous night. "Well" said Dinny "the old sergeant was very busy last night. He came tearing up the bridge and when he saw me he thought I was somebody and when he saw I was nobody, he walked away."

Nora Humphrey's laughter rang out as she related this story from the 1940s and it was lovely to witness the joy and fun she still could grasp from the innocence of the response to her question of so many years ago.

I asked for another song before I took my leave, and in a fine strong and tuneful voice, Nora sang the tragic words of *Kevin Barry* and followed this with the sweet old Irish song *Jimmy mo Mhíle Stór*.

It was with great regret that I learned some time later that Nora Humphreys had passed away, and it was difficult for me to grasp the fact that such a vibrant personality had gone from the world. Nora Humphreys was a custodian of the old memories, and I am very glad indeed that I was afforded the opportunity to meet her and to record her great wealth of stories and songs.

The Late Margaret Kennedy Doughan, Templemore, Co Tipperary

CD No. 22
Time: 46.50
Date Recorded: October 2003

In the autumn of 2003 my wife Jane and I were invited to the Roscrea Conference at Mount St Joseph Abbey to launch the "Irish Life and Lore" collection of recordings in the midlands, which we were very happy to do. George Cunningham, of Roscrea, who organises the annual conferences, suggested that weekend that I travel to Knockanroe near Templemore to meet Margaret Kennedy Doughan. He felt that this was a lady whose memory was crystal clear and whose recollections were worth recording and preserving.

I needed no further prompting and an hour later I was sitting with Margaret and her daughter Kathleen, drinking tea and happily preparing to be entertained and enlightened.

Margaret was born in Waterford city in 1915 and one of her earliest memories was watching through her bedroom window as a battalion of British soldiers marched past en route to drilling manoeuvres, lead by a band and four officers on horseback. This would occur on three mornings a week at 10 a.m. and little Margaret watched in awe as the horses would 'dance' in time to the music.

When she was six years old, due to some unrest in Waterford, Margaret was sent to

Puckaun in Tipperary to stay with her aunt and uncle. Her parents left Waterford shortly afterwards and the family settled in Puckaun.

I prompted her to tell me about her memories of the occupation by the Black and Tans in the Puckaun area, and her voice lowered as she recalled those terrible days. "There was tension everywhere, everybody was terrified" she said, and recalled particularly a small but significant event. A Black and Tan lorry stopped on the road beside her house one day and the men opened fire on a flock of geese in their field, threw the geese onto the lorry and drove away.

People lived in fear and the men would sleep in the haysheds at night, for fear of a raid on their homes, while the women would say the Rosary during the hours of darkness. Margaret's father had a narrow escape one evening when, during a downpour, he took shelter in the house of a relative. His clothes were put to dry by the fire. When the Tans raided the house, they saw the clothes and found Mr Kennedy in bed, and suspicions were aroused. They decided to take him prisoner. Fortunately a local RIC man, who knew Mr Kennedy, was passing by, saw the lorry, and came to investigate. He vouched for the prisoner, whom he knew well, and Margaret's father was allowed return safely to his relieved family.

Those were troubled and dangerous times and Margaret recalled the O'Briens from Nenagh who were shot, Phil Cruise who was taken away but survived his ordeal, the Hogan funeral in Puckaun of which Margaret's childhood memory is very clear. The horse drawn hearse arrived at 12.00 midnight, and the church was opened to receive the remains of the man from Dromineer, who had been shot in Dublin. Amidst the flickering candlelight a small group of women, dressed in black hooded cloaks began to keen, and the terror of the young watcher was still evident in Margaret's voice more than 80 years later.

In 1922 Nora Kennedy, who was Margaret's aunt, boarded in Dromcondra in Dublin, with Nellie Keating, who was a member of Cumann na mBan and relative of Michael Collins. One evening in August, Collins called to the house at around 10.00 p.m., and hung his hat and raincoat in the hall. He was leaving that night on the fateful journey to Cork, and Nellie spent some hours trying to persuade him not to go, because of the inherent danger in making such a trip. Michael was not interested in changing his plans, and when his hat and coat had disappeared from the hallway by morning, Nora Kennedy realised that Collins was on his way to the county of his birth, where he was to tragically meet his fate at Béal na Bláth.

Margaret smiled as she recalled her younger days, and the farming methods and customs of her youth. She spoke of milking and butter making, baking on the open fire, the merits of excellent brown bread, the bacon hung from ceiling hooks, crab apple jelly, mushroom sauce and its making, and the transporting on the bike of wooden butter boxes filled with one pound rolls of butter for the hotel in Roscrea.

We spoke of funerals and wakes and Margaret recalled that before a wake, a member of the family of the deceased would sit all day at the table filling clay pipes with tobacco for the mourners, who would arrive at evening. This reminded her to confide in me that she began smoking at 13 years of age but gave up the habit when, at 18, she fell asleep while smoking and woke to find her armchair on fire. As she pulled the chair outside in great haste she vowed there and then that her relationship with cigarettes would have to be concluded.

Margaret was in her 89th year when I interviewed her, and she was in good health, so I was very saddened to hear a short time later that she had passed away, but the sadness was relieved somewhat by the fact that her clear memories and the sound of her laughter would be preserved and archived.

Before I bade farewell to Margaret and her daughter Kathleen that October afternoon, I was shown an historical collection of handwritten letters. These had been given to Margaret by an elderly relative from Waterford many years before, and had been written by Dr John O'Donovan, the great Celtic scholar of the 1840s. Happily this wonderful collection is now housed with the Royal Irish Academy in Dublin, where it has found a secure home along with many other important documents written by Dr O'Donovan.

As I made my way back to the Conference at Mount St Joseph Abbey that evening, I reflected on a life lived well and happily through dangerous and through peaceful days, and though I was not to know it that evening, a life that would shortly come to an end. I was privileged to have met Margaret Kennedy Doughan and I remember her with great kindness.

The late Margaret Doughan as a young girl with her parents c. 1925

John Knightly, Cashel, Co Tipperary

CD No. 23
Time: 53.57
Date Recorded: September 2005

I had been asked, on several occasions while I was recording in Tipperary, if I was acquainted with John Knightly, the retired schoolteacher from Kerry, now resident in Cashel. I had not had the pleasure of making John's acquaintance so I was determined to rectify the situation. In September 2005, I made contact with John and he readily agreed to talk to me.

John Knightly was born in Annascaul, Co Kerry and lived there till his family moved to Banteer, Co Cork when he was 9 years of age. His father spent 20 years in Annascaul as Station Master and John inherited from him a lifelong interest in railways. He recalled, with a smile, that a friend from Cashel had recently gone to Kerry and brought back a photograph of the viaduct at Lispole. On seeing the photograph John laughed and said "I nearly went to Heaven on that track." As a young boy in 1936 he had been travelling on the train, in the guard's van, along with guard James Ashe. The driver, who had been substituted on that day for the regular driver, lost control of the train, as he had little experience of driving on "that road". The train roared across the viaduct safely and did not stop until it had travelled three quarters of the way to Dingle. Years later, when John was waiting for a friend under Cleary's clock in Dublin, he was approached by a man in railway uniform. This was James Ashe, who enquired if John remembered the day they "nearly went to Heaven."

John also recalled an earlier incident when the engine and some wagons fell off the viaduct, and his father told him that 90% of the adults for miles around came to view the wreckage after that sensational incident.

During the Troubles, in the early 1920s, an event occurred in the area which John feels has never been recorded in detail. His father told him the story of a ship from the Limerick Steamship Company being boarded at Ventry by the IRA. She was carrying flour and Guinness, and was brought by the IRA into Dingle and unloaded. A railway engine and two wagons took the cargo to Annascaul, where the flour was collected by men who arrived with horses and carts from Miltown and Castlemaine. The carts were overloaded, and later many bags of commandeered flour, bearing the legend 'Sunburst Flour' were to be seen discarded inside ditches bordering the roads to Castlemaine. The precious barrels of Guinness were taken at night to Moriarty's pub in Annascaul.

The following Sunday, the parish priest of Annascaul preached a sermon which included the sentence, "the other night, a funeral passed my house at Redcliffe – a funeral of the seventh commandment." The loads of Sunburst Flour and Guinness had been spotted from the presbytery!

John Knightly had a very famous godfather at his christening at Annascaul. The Antarctic explorer, Tom Crean, and his wife Nell were very good friends with the Knightly family and especially with Tom's godson John during his early childhood years. Tom was a great character, full of fun and frivolity, and, indeed, John Knightly's mother, who had six young children under her care, would regularly lock the door if she spied Tom on his way to visit, as he would cause 'ructions' among the children.

Tom Crean would arrive at the station in Annascaul each evening to collect an English newspaper off the Tralee to Dingle train, and if the tide at Blennerville had been high, the train would be delayed for an hour or two, allowing plenty of time for chat about world events. A map of the world was pinned onto the wall of the stationmaster's office in Annascaul. In the 1920s a seaman hijacked a trawler from a port in Africa and steamed down the east coast of the continent. Tom Crean and John's father watched his progress avidly on the map, marking all the ports into which he might steam. Tom Crean knew and marked all the British Navy occupied ports on the African coast. Eventually, the seaman was captured, brought to Portsmouth and fined one shilling.

Crean would never speak of his amazing adventures in the Antarctic. His father explained to John that as the Dingle Peninsula in those days was a hotbed of republicanism, Tom thought it expedient to keep his head down. He and his young godson would often walk, with Crean's two terriers 'Fido' and 'Toby' to the cliffs nearby and one of the dogs, while chasing a rabbit, fell over the cliffs to his death one afternoon. John remembers the deep upset of his godfather as he returned on the following day to bury the little animal.

John has a vivid childhood memory of watching a small plane land on the strand at Inch. On the plane was a nephew of Scott of the Antarctic, who, with some friends, had come to visit Tom Crean at Annascaul. The young boy watched in fascination as the plane was pushed along by a group of men to get it airborne again for its return journey, once the visit was over.

Tom was always known as 'Funny' Crean to John Knightly and his family, and one major disappointment suffered by John during his childhood was the fact that he had never had the opportunity to inspect the frost bitten toes of the great explorer.

The subject of the Irish language was explored during my conversation with John, and he recounted for me the experience of author Ernest Blythe, who came to the Dingle Peninsula to perfect his Irish in the early years of the 20th century. John's father remembered Blythe's arrival in Dingle, where he procured a bicycle from Brid de Barra, and set off with a letter of introduction to all the teachers in the area. His plan was to live in a family home as a labourer, and work for his keep and learn the language. He was having great difficulty finding a home willing to take him in, as people were very poor with barely sufficient food for themselves. He wrote to An Seabhac, and on its arrival in Dublin the letter was read by Tom Ashe from Kinard, near Dingle. He wrote to Blythe and told him to go to Kinard as his brother Greg had gone to America, and his bed in the loft was vacant. Ernest Blythe did as instructed and stayed in Kinard for almost six months, perfecting his Irish and developing a great love for the area.

John Knightly left his native county when, in 1949, he arrived in Cashel to begin his teaching career, having previously trained in St Patrick's College, Dromcondra in Dublin. His career in teaching began in a small Junior Boys school, which was, he declared "the happiest place ever." The Principal of the school was Kerryman Frank Egan, from Castlegregory. Having taught for 20 years at the school, John Knightly was appointed Principal.

His favourite subject, during his life of teaching, was Irish and John recalled that his father in Annascaul had little fluency in the language. As a child, John would watch as fishermen from the Blasket Islands arrived in Annascaul by train from Dingle. They came to collect willows for the making of lobster pots, and would spend a few days cutting and binding the willows. They would then load them onto the train for Dingle, travel on to Dunquin, and onto the namhógs to sail to the island. While in Annascaul they were given lodgings by local farmers, and John remembers his father's difficulty in trying to converse with the islanders who spoke only in their native tongue.

John had many interesting facts to relate regarding boat building on the Blaskets, and the origins of the namhógs, and I realised that this was not the time to stem the flow of such recollections. I sat where I was, enthralled, and continued to record this wonderful man.

Wedding photograph of Antartic explorer Tom Crean and his wife Nell

John Knightly, Cashel, Co Tipperary

CD No. 24
Time: 41.03
Date Recorded: September 2005

John Knightly is a man well known and loved throughout the length and breadth of Tipperary, and in September 2005 I spent several contented hours in his company at his home in Cashel, where I recorded some of his great memories and recollections.

In the latter part of our conversation John recalled, with pleasure, his school teaching career in Cashel, which was a time of great happiness for him. He recalled that he would, when possible, teach songs and recitations appropriate to the local area. He sang a snatch of *An Spailpín Fánach* which reminded us that the Spailpíns would come from the poorer lands of Kerry and West Cork to find work in the lush fields of Tipperary. During his teaching days he always felt that geography was a subject which was "on the wrong path". He feels that the geography of one's own townland and county should be taught initially and afterwards, the geography of the wider world. Due to the method of teaching geography, he feels that often the local young children had little knowledge of, or interest in, the ancient Rock of Cashel, which stands proudly in their native place.

He told a lovely story about a visit he made to the local school in Annascaul, Co Kerry some years ago. He was accompanying his elderly father on a trip back to his home place, and on passing the school, his father told him that he had heard that the present Principal was a relative of the family. John had never met this man, and thought that perhaps a little bit of fun could be had on the day when the children were due to begin their school holidays.

Off he went to the Principal's class, knocked on the door and said "Is mise an Roinn Cigire" (I am the class inspector), at which the Principal explained that they were a little relaxed due to the fact that the school was closing for holidays on that day. John Knightly, speaking in Irish, began to ask the children the meaning of the local placenames, which he rattled off to the amazement of the Principal. He then asked to see the school register. On opening the page on the year 1932, he pointed out, for the Principal, the name of John Knightly, who had been brought to the school on his very first day by his godfather, Antarctic explorer, Tom Crean. The school Principal, the children and John Knightly all had a good laugh later at the "Cigire" who had such an intimate knowledge of local placenames, having spent many happy childhood years living in the village.

John had many interesting little stories to relate about Tom Crean, and he feels that one story has not previously been recorded. It concerns one evil night on board the "James Caird" en route to South Georgia, when Crean was at the tiller, and the rest of the crew were sheltering under the canvas decking. Crean cried out for a hot drink, and one man lit the primus stove, another held a mug of ice over the flame until the ice melted, then spooned in some cocoa and passed it to the perished Tom Crean, who gulped it down. Gasping, he remarked that the cocoa tasted very hot, and it was only then the crew noticed that they had given him a mug of hot water mixed with curry powder!

In 1988 a plaque was erected in Annascaul to the memory of Tom Crean and on that evening, a lecture on the Polar Expedition was given in a Dingle hotel by an Oxford professor named Headland. He illustrated his lecture with 60 wonderful slides and afterwards announced that he was presenting the slides to the Dingle library. Some time later, John, who was to give a series of talks to some of the Tipperary Historical Societies, attempted to trace these slides, but his quest was unsuccessful. He feels that sadly the slides may have been mislaid in the Dingle Hotel on the night of the presentation in 1988.

We spoke of communications and of how contact was maintained among buyers and sellers of produce in Kerry in the early days of the 20th century. Rabbits were caught by the dozen during the winter months on Inch Island near Annascaul, and sent by train to Paris. Fish were landed in Dingle, and as there was just one telephone in the town, the local agents would queue up at the post office to ring their agents in England to decide on the consignment which was then sent by train and boat to Crewe Junction for further distribution throughout southern England.

The first travelling creamery to come to Kerry was closely watched by the young John Knightly from his vantage point on the shoulders of this father, Robert. The creamery came from Rathmore where the manager was Mr Blackwell, who had previously worked in Ardmayle, close to where John now lives in Cashel.

In the 1930s a professor from Trinity College in Dublin came on holiday to Annascaul. He had a great interest in the development of turf, and went up to the top of Glenagealt to examine the turf banks at Slieve. He became friendly with Robert Knightly, and later sent him 20 haversacks, which he requested be filled with turf samples, as he wanted to test the turf for calorific value. John and his father set off one evening on the train from Annascaul. At various places they hopped out and distributed the haversacks to the local farmers. The bags were duly filled, and were picked up by train at an appointed time some days later. The samples made their way to Dublin and the mission was thus accomplished. The academic from Trinity College later became Chairman of the Turf Development Board, the predecessor to Bord na Mona.

I could have listened to John Knightly's recollections far into the night, but time, as always, worked her thieving ways and I had to take my leave. It was a real pleasure for me to spend some time in the company of this man of learning who was so kind and generous with his time and with his great wealth of knowledge.

The late Brother Peter McGovern, Mount St Joseph Abbey, Roscrea, Co Tipperary

CD No. 25:
Time: 49.47
Date Recorded: October 2003

One crisp Autumn evening in 2003, as I walked through the grounds of Mount St Joseph Abbey in Roscrea, the bell began to toll as if to call me to my appointment with Brother Peter McGovern, who was waiting for me indoors. I had previously met Brother Peter briefly and had become intrigued by his gentleness and sense of humour, so here was my opportunity to sit with him and listen to his musings and recollections of a long and varied life.

Since our meeting in 2003, Brother Peter has passed away in his 98th year, and while I was very saddened to hear of his death, I was also pleased that his voice, his whistle playing and his songs had been recorded and would now be carefully preserved.

Brother Peter began our conversation by telling me that he was born in February 1907, near Belleek, Co Fermanagh. As a young man he spent fifteen happy years working as an agent for Belleek Potteries, but always at the back of his mind, his vocation was becoming more evident. He described how he would often wake at night to think about it and it was a constant presence in his life.

He joined the army, but his stay was of short duration – he was an unlikely prospect for soldiering! He decided to try his hand at smuggling a few cattle across the border, but was caught by the Gardai and when he appeared in Court the Justice gave him an option of a £10 fine or a fortnight in Mountjoy. He chose the latter – a richer experience. While in Mountjoy he met and befriended playwright Brendan Behan, who had been incarcerated due to his activities with the IRA.

Before he decided to join the Cistercian Order in Roscrea, he had had a girlfriend, but was somewhat undecided about his feelings for her, and eventually, at the age of 40 he decided on the path which was to lead to his religious life in Roscrea.

I asked Brother Peter about the jobs he was instructed to undertake when he first joined the Order, and he laughed heartily as he told me that the command he got from Fr Patrick was "Look at the roads out there!" and 60 years later he was still employed mending the roads, and nobody had ever checked on him!

When Brother Peter began his days at Mount St Joseph Abbey there were eight novices in residence, and he and Bernard Hayes, a Kerryman, were slow to learn the monastic sign language which was used for communication, owing to the vow of silence. One day, Bernard and Peter decided that they would "talk for a few days and chuck it after that". As Brother Peter said, he had the privilege of always being caught, and so it was on this occasion.

He was always very interested in art and spent a lot of his time drawing faces in an abstract style. He showed me one interesting example of the faces of poet Patrick Kavanagh and a friend. Since childhood he had been drawing, and he recalled, with a chuckle, that his teacher would always push his sketch book to the bottom of the pile when the inspector was due to call!

He had a great love of animals and he could regularly be seen working with Ben, his faithful donkey, which had been bought at a fair in Waterford for £200. He and Ben were much photographed by tourists and he declared ruefully that if they were at the Cliffs of Moher, they would be earning £1 a photograph.

Brother Peter wrote a few plays over the years and his particular favourite was "Paddy Reilly from Ballyjamesduff." He explained the origin of this play by describing a trip he made home from Dublin one early morning in an Austin 7. In Ballyjamesduff, he came across a young man, going from house to house, singing the song, at 8.00 a.m. Brother Peter got out of the car, and followed the singer around the streets until he had memorised the song, and immediately on his return home, he began to write the play.

I was keen to know if he had ever gone to Lough Derg on pilgrimage and again he dissolved into laughter as he described an occasion when he hitch-hiked to the Holy Island from Roscrea, and was given a lift in a jeep. All went well until after a mile or two it became evident that the journey would take all day as the driver never exceeded

12 miles an hour. Eventually Brother Peter took a little nap in the back of the jeep to shorten the journey towards the place of pilgrimage.

I was told a funny story about Brother Peter's prowess on the football field on one particular occasion, and he took great delight in demonstrating for me his cunning moves which led him to score a goal on that memorable and far-ff day.

He had his beloved tin whistle in his hands during our conversation, and now he played the first verse of *She Moved Through the Fair* and then he sang that haunting ballad, and followed by *Paddy Reilly from Ballyjamesduff* sung in a sweet and tuneful voice,

Oh the grass it is green around Ballyjamesduff,
And the blue sky hangs over it all."

As I prepared to take my leave and the evening darkened outside the windows, I asked Brother Peter how he feels his monastic life has been lived and he answered "contentment sums it up. Nothing is too great for love, nothing too little."

This belief, I feel, encapsulated the character of the late Brother Peter McGovern, a man of talent, humour, holiness and humility.

The late Br. Peter McGovern hard at work with the help of his faithful Ben.

LATE BROTHER PETER

It was with great sadness that the death occurred over the weekend of Bother Peter, one of the most popular monks to have ever passed through the gates of Mount Saint Joseph's. Br Peter who hails from Fermanagh,entered monastery life in 1947. He was professed in 1949 and remained a loyal and devoted servant of the Abbey for the rest of his life. Br Peter loved nature and it was no great surprise that much of his time was devoted to the famous Monastery farm. He was also a man who enjoyed all aspects of art, but perhaps the image people must conjure up when Br Peter's name is mentioned is the familiar sight of Br Peter leading his Donkey and Cart with his famous tin whistle eased between his lips. Br Peter loved music and loved the tin whistle in particular. No doubt he was a unique character and will be sadly missed by all those who had the pleasure of knowing this great man, who died in his ninety seventh year. Dom Kevin Daly celebrated Br Peter's funeral on Monday last and he was laid to rest immediately afterwards in the beautiful surrounds of the adjoining cemetery. May he rest in peace.

"Guardian" newspaper tribute.

Tom Wallace, Ardmayle, Cashel, Co Tipperary

CD No. 26:
Time: 43.10
Date Recorded: August 2005

As I drove from Cashel towards the townland of Ardmayle in the parish of Boherlahan, I reflected on the poetic nature of these placenames and on the lush beauty of the August countryside. I was on my way to meet Tom Wallace at his home in Ardmayle, where a fine Tipperary welcome awaited me.

I had previously heard that Charles Bianconi had lived nearby at Longfield House in earlier times and Tom explained that, as a young penniless man, Bianconi came from Italy to work as a peddler around the roads of Tipperary and elsewhere. One day as he journeyed from Thurles he climbed up to the Moate at Ardmayle and saw the glorious Longfield House in the distance, surrounded by its large estate. He was a young man of vision and determination and he vowed that the estate would some day be his. He became "the man who put Ireland on wheels", by setting up a coach business in Cashel, and as the years went by and success followed success, the day finally arrived when he unlocked the door at Longfield House and made the place his own.

Tom related an interesting fact about one of Bianconi's rules for his stations, where horses were changed overnight. Anybody who lived at the station was not allowed to keep hens, as the pragmatic Bianconi felt that the oats provided for the horses would also inevitably be used as poultry feed. Charles Bianconi is buried at Boherlahan, as is his son in law Morgan John O'Connell, a nephew of "The Liberator" Daniel O'Connell of Derrynane in Kerry.

When Tom Wallace was growing up in Ardmayle he was greatly influenced by a man named John O'Connell, who was born in 1904. John worked with local farmers and had an abiding interest in local history. He lived through all the turmoil of the early years of the 20th century and a photograph exists showing John and his six siblings all dressed in the uniform of the Blueshirts in the 1930s. He told Tom about the odd skirmish which would occur between the Blueshirts and the mainly republican population of the area. During the Blueshirt meetings in a shed roofed in galvanised iron, stones would regularly be pelted onto the roof. He had a vivid memory of a meeting addressed by General O'Duffy, leader of the Blueshirts, in Cashel, after which a riot erupted.

John O'Connell would often sketch for his young listener the details of the class distinction which prevailed in his youth. During a threshing, when it was time for dinner, the woman of the house would stand at the door to direct the farmers and their sons to the parlour, and the labourers, such as himself, to the kitchen. On fair days in Thurles, the household would arise at 4 a.m. to walk the cattle to the fair, and the labourers would eat alone in the kitchen apart from the farmers and their families.

John was an expert at tracing and he knew all the families whose names are engraved on the headstones in Ardmayle graveyard. He had been a member of the Pioneer Total Abstinence Association all his life, and Tom Wallace also followed this path. He remembers with fondness the early 1960s and going to dances in Cricklewood and Holloway in London, where no bar was available, and minerals were the only thirst quenchers on offer.

Tom recalls clearly the arrival of the first tractors in the area and marvels at the extraordinary changes that have taken place in farming during his lifetime. He recalls his schooldays when he and his friends would call to a neighbour's house on the way home from school on the day of the threshing, in the sure and certain knowledge that a few bottles of lemonade awaited them to cheer them on their journey home.

I enquired about the placenames in the area and was pleased to hear that Tom knew not only the placenames but the fieldnames as well. He mentioned in particular the Mass Path Field, across which hundreds of people would walk to Mass from Longfield to Boherlahan, crossing the Suir at a low point, and up to the Double Ditch. Work is being undertaken on placenames at present, I was told, for the local Historical Journal – a very worthwhile project indeed.

We talked of local bohereens under threat due to road widening and of a road to the bog at Ballymore which is now abandoned. Tom recalls cutting turf at Ballymore where now the bog is no more.

The village of Ardmayle was a thriving spot during Tom's younger days. The creamery sent prize-winning butter to London and Tom handed me a lovely photograph from the 1950s showing his uncle, Michael Wallace, with a cart loaded with churns for the trip to the creamery. The railway was busy and the village shop did a steady trade. Later the creamery was amalgamated with Mitchelstown Creamery, the school was amalgamated with Boherlahan School and the railway closed in the early 1950s. Just as in many other rural areas of Ireland, the railway was a major loss to the area.

Tom's school days at Ardmayle were happy and as he lived a hundred yards from the school, he was spared the weary miles of walking many of his contemporaries endured. The hours of learning were punctuated by the sounds from outside the windows, and when the clip clop of the horses' hooves could be heard on the way back to the creamery for the buttermilk, every youngster knew it was 2.30 p.m. and his incarceration would soon be over for the day. When school closed at 3.00 p.m. the first port of call would be the creamery for a free glass of buttermilk, but only if the manager, Pat Harrington was absent, as he feared for the childrens' safety in the environs of the creamery. I could almost see the small boys relish the cold buttermilk, more delicious than ice cream, on a hot summer afternoon after the long hours of study, discipline and diligence.

I regretfully left Ardmayle and my friend Tom Wallace on that afternoon, almost believing that I too had tasted the sweet buttermilk on those far off summer days in the village of Ardmayle in South Tipperary.

The late Michael Wallace, creamery bound c. 1950

Back Row L to R: Mick O'Neill, Tom Wallace, John O'Connell & Mic Wallace
Front Row L to R: Tom Hennesy, Bill Wallace, Dick Hennesy & Peter Tyrel
Photographed at the Moate at Ardmayle c. 1940

Threshing at Freighduff c. 1940

Back Row L to R: Jim Kinnane (partly hidden), Paddy Devane, Tom Kinnane, Martin Hackett, Jim Mc Grath, Tom Wallace, Billy Burns, Danny Murphy & Willie O'Connell.

Front Row L to R: Mary Myers (with basket), William Finnal, Billy Murphy Jnr., Mick Maher & Mrs Murphy (Pump Hill)

Peggy Geraghty, Monroe, Newtown, Co Tipperary

CD No. 27
Time: 59.51
Date Recorded: September 2005

My first meeting with Siobhán Geraghty, the Heritage Officer for North Tipperary, took place in 2004 and since that time she has helped me in numerous ways in my efforts to record the recollections of the people of Tipperary. In September 2005 she introduced me to her mother, Peggy Geraghty, at the lovely old family home at Monroe, and I was fascinated to learn that initially, the house had been built as a school.

In 1841 the building was erected for use as a school, and after the famine, in the late 1840s, it was written into the deeds that the building was to be used as a Protestant chapel or as a residence for a Protestant clergyman. Up to the mid 20th century it was used weekly as a chapel and a local family lived upstairs and acted as caretakers of the property. It became derelict after the 1950s, was bought by an Englishman for use as a holiday home, and in 1974, the Geraghty family made the place their own. It is now a home imbued with a sense of peace, warmth and comfort. When I mentioned the book-lined walls all round me, Peggy laughed as she pointed out that the family is addicted to reading and though occasionally they make a decision to refrain from visiting bookshops, somebody invariably sneaks out and gleefully comes back with an armful of reading material.

Peggy Geraghty was born in 1927 and grew up in County Mayo, in a family of seven girls and one boy. She was never very impressed with the standard of teaching at the local school, and when she was twelve years old, she was sent as a boarder to the Presentation convent in Tuam. At this time she had never travelled further than the local village, which was three miles from her home, had never been on a bus or seen the sea. Boarding school was a very strange place for a young girl, who had grown up in a large and close family circle, but Peggy became settled there, and grew to love many of the nuns.

The students at the convent were immersed in the Catholic traditions, were all enrolled as Children of Mary and were regularly visited by missionaries. When the time came for Peggy to leave the convent, she had made the decision that her future lay as a missionary sister, working at a leper colony.

The Presentation Order had a Novitiate at Castleconnell, and it was here that Peggy encountered for the first time the narrow-minded belief that the will of a young novice had to be broken in order to prepare her for the religious life. She laughs now as she recalls the time when she was appointed sacristan, and one of her duties was to ensure that the Sanctuary lamp was kept lit at all times. The penance for failing in this duty was to kneel on the refectory floor and repent, as all the other novices and mistress ate their meal. This penance became customary in Peggy's life as the sanctuary lamp regularly went out, much to her mystification and dismay. All was explained when early one morning, before 5.45 a.m., she crept down to the chapel to check that the lamp was lighting, only to discover the novice mistress quenching it! This, Peggy felt, was a lesson in humility for the young novice, but was an obvious source of great resentment as well.

It was decided that she would study for a science degree, and when the happy years of study were completed, she was sent to Newcastle to complete her Diploma in Education, having first taken her final vows. No sooner had she arrived in Newcastle, than she was summoned to Matlock to teach for one year, after which she was to complete her Diploma. The Reverend Mother at Matlock was none other than the former novice mistress at Castleconnell, with whom Peggy had a less than happy relationship, and a miserable year for the young nun ensued.

Peggy endured the hardships of those twelve months at Matlock, returned to Newcastle and completed her Diploma in Education. She loved her teaching practice and loved the children who had a great warmth and friendliness, but she was in great difficulty regarding her vocation to the religious life. She discussed the situation with her confessor, who was very supportive, and who told her to write to the Superior General and to Rome. She also wrote to her sister, Dilly, and told her of her doubts, and was to learn that her mother was less than happy to hear of this turn of events.

Eventually, at 25 years of age, she was released from her vows and left the convent with "no money, and no idea how to behave." Her family sent her some clothes and the fare home. She stayed for a while with her sister, Mary, and took a part-time teaching job in Dublin as she savoured her new-found freedom. After some time she took a teaching post in Yorkshire, at a small boarding school, and on her return to Dublin for Christmas, she went with some friends for a night out to a singing pub, her second visit ever to such an establishment. While enjoying several double Benedictines she met a young man who asked to see her again, and the Céili in the Mansion House on St Stephen's night was the agreed meeting place. The following day a telegram arrived from her mother, pleading with her to come home for Christmas, and on her return to Dublin some days later, having missed her appointment at the Mansion House, the young man, who had heard of her trip home, was there to meet her at the station. Vincent Geraghty and Peggy became husband and wife one year later.

They were to teach in London and Norwich for the next 13 years, during which time their daughter Siobhán was born. As the unrest in the North of Ireland took its toll, the welcome for Irish people in England began to evaporate, and the Geraghty family decided it was time to return to Ireland.

In 1974 they spotted the old schoolhouse and chapel in Monroe, fell in love with it, and bought it for a good price, as in the locality it was thought to be haunted, a suggestion which prompted a hearty chuckle from Peggy.

She studied for a postgraduate degree in Philosophy, and was to teach the first intake of students to the College in Limerick. She taught there for many fulfilling years and on her retirement, took up a fascinating hobby. She decided to learn to paint icons, wonderful examples of which were hanging on the walls of the house. Peggy told me that the materials used and the techniques of icon painting have not changed for over 100 years, and she described in detail the process of painting in tempera, the use of gesso and the gilding.

We climbed up the narrow staircase in the house and found Vincent hard at work, hanging some of the earlier icons on the walls, in preparation for some guests who were coming to stay the following afternoon.

I was keen to know what were Peggy Geraghty's feelings on the Catholic religion following her earlier experiences as a young nun. She smiled at me as she said that she had rejected religion for many years, but in 1993 she attended a retreat in Glenstal, and following that profound experience she felt herself at peace with her faith once again.

Peggy and Vincent Geraghty live happily and contentedly in their lovely old home at Monroe, at peace with the world in all its great variety and I wish them many more years of industry, health and happiness.

Peggy Geraghty relaxes at home

Exterior view of the Geraghty home at Monroe

Bridget Malone, Ballycarridoge, Portroe, Co Tipperary

CD No. 28

Time: 71.31

Date Recorded: September 2005

The September sun cast its slanting rays over the lush green fields around Ballycarridoge, as I drove to meet Bridget Malone at her lovely old home. The house was built in 1930 to replace an earlier thatched building, and the yard is sheltered by a barn and cow house, both built of old cut stone.

Bridget invited me to stroll with her around the nearby fields, and as we walked she told me that the local creamery was built in 1914 but prior to this people would make their own butter. She described the utensils used for the making of this delicious food, and recalled and named the many pieces of equipment in everyday use prior to farm mechanisation. She also described in detail for me the cutting, footing and drying of the turf on the mountain.

Bridget Malone's first home was nearby in a place called Lacamore, which means 'the big hillside'. Her parents were William McKeogh and Kate Hickey, who had been neighbours, and in his early youth, William was employed at the local slate quarries. At one time over 700 people worked there, but by 1923, when the quarries were taken over by Barney O'Driscoll from Cork, the numbers employed were approximately 200.

With the advent of asbestos, the quarrying of slate became financially uncompetitive and the quarries ceased to function.

Bridget's early schooling was undertaken in a schoolhouse "as big as a nice haybarn." It was divided into two rooms by a partition, and as there was no ceiling, many a shower of freezing hailstones found its way onto the heads of the children below. I wondered aloud about the effects of the cold in such a building, and was told of the absolute necessity of strong boots and knitted stockings. Despite these barriers against the chill the children were plagued by chilblains and Bridget remembers walking home from school on small feet numbed by the cold.

Her teacher was John McGrath, whom Bridget remembers with fondness. During the reign of the Black and Tans he was taken away in one of their lorries, but was returned unharmed. During this dramatic interlude the school was run by another teacher, Mrs Malone. Bridget remembers the lorries of the Tans on the roads, and on one occasion while walking to school she turned back for home in fear for her safety. She recalled that when "the boys" were felling trees across the roads to block the Tans' lorries, local men would be taken out on the lorries by the Crown Forces to cut up the trees to open the roads again.

Bridget suggested that a cup of tea might be welcome, so we made our way indoors and, as we walked along she recalled that the Rosary was said every night in all the local houses in her youth. All the family were expected to be "in for the Rosary" and this was a clever way of keeping track of the young people and their movements, as parents, in those days, were normally very strict. Entertainment consisted of card playing or dancing in local houses, and people thought nothing of walking miles for entertainment. She often heard about young men who would work all day on the local farms, and walk in the evening to the Shannon to swim – a fair distance indeed.

All the news of note in the neighbourhood was discussed and dissected while waiting each day at the creamery with the ass and car, but once tractors arrived, regretfully all this fascinating exchange of news became a thing of the past.

The daily work of the women in those far off days was recalled, as Bridget described the baking, the cleaning, the washing and the drawing of water. She has a clear memory of early summer days at Lacamore, where, close by the house under the shade of a tree by a waterfall, a bucket, holding butter, would be placed in the water to keep it cool. Potatoes and turnips were also washed there and brought back to the kitchen.

She spoke lovingly of the special jobs all the children had to do after school each day, though the tasks may not have been too beloved at the time. The children were despatched to collect turf and sticks, collect eggs, bring water, weed turnips and pick potatoes. Her maternal grandmother remains dear in Bridget's memory. She was a lady of great industry, forever sewing and making suits for all her young sons.

We spoke of the sugán chairs, dressers and settles which stood in all the homes of old, of the local carpenters who made them with patience and skill, and of all the goods which were available for purchase in Portroe village in times past. Bridget named out the houses in the village, remembering the barracks, the doctors' house, the district nurse's house, the church, the five pubs and groceries, the shoemaker, the two butchers, the drapery and the post office. There were also two very busy blacksmiths in the area, who, apart from tending to the horses, would also repair and make farm machinery, gates and the cranes used for holding pots over the open fires.

Bridget was employed for ten years by Mrs Jones in a drapery shop in Portroe, and this shop could supply almost anything a person would need from cradle to grave. One could buy hardware, shoes and boots, cattle medicines, shrouds, baby wear and bottles, bluestone for the spraying of potatoes, turnip seed, bacon, flour, meal and bran, sugar, tea and much more besides. There were suit lengths to be bought and brought to the tailor, there were washboards and basins for washing and ewers and basins for the ablutions.

Everything followed a strict routine in the shop. A special day was set aside for weighing the goods and everything had its own place. People had time to sit and chat after their shopping, and perhaps have a couple of 'mediums'. Bridget was able to enlighten me on the almost exact proportions of a 'medium': more than a half pint and less than a pint!

She spoke of her experiences of wakes in earlier days, of the superstitions which were rife around the countryside, of cures and customs, and while she declared that she sometimes finds it difficult to remember recent events, things which happened long ago "have root taken", and are simple for her to recall.

As I prepared to take my leave I got the feeling that Bridget Malone was only just beginning to get into her stride with her recollections, and I decided that this was a great lady who was alive with memories whom I would definitely visit again on my next trip to Portroe.

Pat Moloney, Ballycarridoge, Portroe, Co Tipperary

CD No. 29
Time: 52.52
Date Recorded: September 2005

Pat Moloney was sitting comfortably by the gate at the entrance to his property at Ballycarridoge as I approached one evening in the autumn of 2005. His smile and wave of welcome warmed my heart. The All-Ireland hurling final was being played that day in Croke Park between Cork and Galway but as the Premier County had no part to play on this occasion, Pat was happy to spend some time in conversation with me.

I had been introduced to him by Matthew Malone, whose mother, Bridget I had previously recorded, and as we settled ourselves to begin, Pat told me that he was now over 86 years of age. He had moved to his present house 30 years previously, having lived in the nearby stone built, thatched family home. He was regarded as a good scholar in his early days, being particularly adept at mathematics, and though some thought was given to the idea of a career as a teacher, he left school at 14, as his help was needed on the farm at home. His father made ends meet by working part time for the council, with his horse on the roads, and the payment for this was eight shillings a day. This helped pay the rent and rates which fell due twice a year. The family owned three cows, and later this number was increased when Pat took over the farm.

He told me that he always had a great love for the outdoor life, and for many years he spent a 16 week term working at the quarry for the council, before the busy period on the farm began. He was a marvellous ploughman with his horses, and he could make drills "as straight as the edge of a table." He recalled that his father had been just as exact and his uncle "even worse".

I asked Pat about the local placenames and field names, which he had no trouble in listing off. He spoke about the Mass Rock at the Field of Johns. Mass was said here three years ago, and Pat says he knows every inch of the Mass Rock as he often had to take great care when ploughing around it during his farming days.

Our conversation meandered onto to the subject of explosives, as due to the workings at the nearby quarries, Pat, and his father before him, had some experience in this field. He assured me that gelignite was not too good for splitting a great trunk of a tree, as the timber would chip into pieces – powder was the man for the job!

In years gone by Pat Moloney would begin killing pigs for the family's use, and for the neighbours, from November onwards each year. He would kill ten to twelve pigs a year and I was amazed to hear that he still salts a pig in a barrel for his own use. He has killed pigs weighing up to 32 stone, and explained that it is a very exact procedure, which includes the use of particular knives to cut up the meat on the evening following the killing. In early days, prior to electrification, the meat would be cut up by candlelight with very 'edgy' knives, and fingers were regularly put at grave risk.

Making the puddings from the pig's blood was a trade in itself and Pat maintained that there was no food to equal a good pork-steak. He paid great tribute to the women of earlier times who were geniuses in his view, who could turn their hands to any job. He still has his mother's sewing machine and, with a laugh, told me that he could still employ it if a "crack came on his breeches". We talked of thatching, of lime washing, of the dresser and settle bed in all the country homes of old, of the staple diet and the big families.

"Like the fox, you'd travel to the platform" laughed Pat as he recalled the nights of fun he and his friends enjoyed as they cycled miles to the platforms to dance till the small hours. He named some of the musicians he remembered, giving special mention to Ned "Shiner" Quigley. The parish priest was sometimes less than pleased with the high spirits, but Pat maintained that he could do little about it, as the people of the parish kept him going financially and he had to "tread lightly".

The well in the 'Goosepark' gave beautiful water he told me, which would be collected in white enamel buckets for the house, and the rain water was also collected in barrels for washing. Pat recalled cutting turf on the mountain during World War II and later going to auctions to buy a couple of trees which were cut with a crosscut and drawn home for firewood during the winter. Very little coal was burned, and if it was needed, the journey to Nenagh was made with the horse and car, which would be weighed on the weighbridge before and after loading to determine the price to be paid.

I enquired if there were many storytellers in the area during earlier years and Pat laughed merrily as he declared that "the only storytellers were liars." He made the point that unlike storytelling, the working of pisheogs was prevalent. He knew of a woman who would be very busy at May Eve, and on one occasion Pat was shocked to see a piece of fresh pig meat fall out of his cock of hay. He suffered losses with his cattle that year, and went to the local Canon and asked him to say a Mass. The Canon agreed, saying "we'll see who has the most power." The Mass was duly said, and no more trouble came to Pat Moloney's door. He said that in far off days people from Tipperary would sometimes travel to County Clare to meet Biddy Early, who could tell them the name of the person who was working the pisheogs.

As I bade my farewell to Pat, he settled himself again by the gate to watch the world go about its business, and I decided a happier man would be very hard indeed to find on a long day's march.

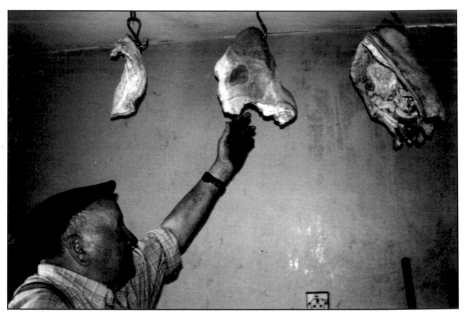

Pat Moloney checks his stocks for winter

William Hayes, Carraig Hill, Roscrea, Co Tipperary

CD No. 30
Time: 74.27
Date Recorded: September 2005

A question often asked of me in the homes of Tipperary was "have you met Willie Hayes yet?" and until a September day in 2005, I had not had that pleasure. In eager anticipation I made my way to Carraig Hill, which overlooks the town of Roscrea, introduced myself to William, was warmly welcomed and invited to sit in the sunshine and enjoy the view of historic Roscrea.

William Hayes has lived a most interesting and varied life, and now devotes most of his time to historical research and to writing. His journey to this happy stage of his life began at Rathcoole, near Fethard, where he was born into the family of eight children of Margaret Mary Walsh of Clogheen and Tom Hayes of Rathcoole. His parents married during the summer of 1922, at the height of the Civil War, and a few weeks before Michael Collins was shot. The Hayes family had no involvement with the politics of the day, but William's mother's family, the Walshs, included two members who were imprisoned at Ballykinlar during the War of Independence. The Walsh home at Clogheen was regarded as a 'safe house', as it was set back from the road in a quiet area between Clogheen and Cahir, and its seclusion was availed of by Dan Breen and some of his associates on at least one occasion.

Margaret Mary Walsh is remembered with great kindness by her son William, who recalled her avid interest in nature and in old and historic buildings and places. In fact, it was she who accompanied the young William Hayes on his very first visit to Holy Cross Abbey. This visit, and his mother's abiding interest in local history, may have been the spur which William needed to crystallise his passion for history and writing in adult life. When I enquired if he had been inspired by his earliest schoolteacher, with a wry smile he replied in the negative. He was educated initially by the Patrician Brothers in Fethard and progressed to secondary education at a new school run by the Brothers, which had opened just as he finished his primary school days.

In his teenage years he became friendly with a local curate, Fr Christopher Lee, through their mutual interest in hunting and shooting, and this friendship had some bearing on William's decision to join the priesthood. He attended the Diocesan Seminary in Thurles and later Maynooth, and was ordained in 1955. During his time in Maynooth, Archbishop Patrick O'Donnell of Brisbane, who was born in Fethard, had visited the college and suggested to William that he consider coming to minister in Brisbane after his ordination. In 1955 the young priest set sail for Australia. He worked in a parish near Brisbane for six very happy years, until in 1961, Archbishop Morris decided that his ministry was required in the Diocese of Cashel and Emly.

His first appointment was as Chaplain to the Presentation Convent in Cashel, which incorporated an orphanage for girls, ranging in age from 3 to 16 years. A further appointment as curate at Cappawhite followed and in 1966, he was appointed as curate and administrator at Holy Cross. Here began a very significant period in William's life, as the idea began to take root that the Abbey at Holy Cross could, and should, be restored. The local parish church, built in 1832, was in a poor state of repair, and needed extensive remedial work which was set to begin shortly. The senior architect at the Office of Public Works was approached with the proposition that Holy Cross Abbey could be restored instead, for use as the parish church. This proposal, if implemented, would be very costly indeed, but with the enthusiastic backing of Archbishop Morris, the decision to go ahead with the work was made in 1969.

William was closely involved with the negotiations with local families regarding the removal of remains which had lain buried in the interior of the Abbey since 1780, for reburial outside. He clearly recalls the generosity and graciousness of the families involved. Once the reburials had been completed the restoration on the building began and the work continued until the Abbey opened in 1975. William wrote the booklet *Holy Cross Abbey: An Illustrated History and Guide*, which was published in 1974, and which went on sale at the Abbey office initially for half-a-crown, and later at five

Mass at the newly restored Holy Cross Abbey, 1977

shillings a copy. All proceeds went towards the restoration fund. Fundraising began all over Tipperary and Archbishop Morris went to America to raise funds from the Irish people there. The State forwarded, on loan, the salaries of the workers on the restoration and all this money was later paid back through the funds raised.

In 1977, William was appointed to Newport Parish and lived at Birdhill, where many of his free hours were happily spent fishing on the Shannon from his little rowboat. He loved his time in the parish, and became involved in setting up an historical group, from which grew the present very active Historical Society. The area around Newport is steeped in history and William loved talking to the local people about the origins of the place, and so the seed was sown for his book, *Newport, Co Tipperary: The Town, Its Courts and Gaols*. He has especially fond memories of the late Nora Humphreys, Paddy Coffey, the late Mike Hassett of Birdhill, Principal of Birdhill School, Michael Collins and veterinary surgeon Packie Ryan, all of whom are and were a mine of valuable information on their native place.

The sun was fleeing on its long journey westwards, so we retreated indoors and sat awhile in William's workplace. He described for me the major decision he made to re-direct his life, to leave the priesthood and to marry his beloved Maureen. They both felt after their marriage that a different environment would be conducive to a successful and happy future, so they spent nearly six years in Australia, both working as teachers in Brisbane. In 1986, with their young son, they returned home, due to the failing health of older member of both of their families. William smiles as he recalls introducing his son to the fields and hills of Tipperary, and the warm welcome the family received everywhere they went.

A new stage of life now began as William explained that having been a priest in Ireland for so long, "I felt dislodged, so to speak. There was a disconnection." He was still fully involved with his Catholic faith but was removed from the structure of the priesthood. He began work in the supervision of a number of FÁS schemes, and one of the schemes involved the cleaning of the graveyard at Templemore. This work led to his research on the graves there and eventually to his book, *The Old Church and Graveyard at Templemore* published in 1995. 1998 saw the publication of his book *Tipperary in the year of Rebellion 1798*. He describes the reign of terror conducted by Thomas Fitzgerald, the High Sheriff of Tipperary, against any sign of insurrection in the county in 1798. He became known as "Flogger" Fitzgerald because of the savage methods he liked to employ against the insurgents.

Congregation at mass at the restored Holy Cross Abbey, 1977

The next major work undertaken by William was in conjunction with George Cunningham, also from Roscrea, and as he showed me the three wonderful volumes which comprise *The Parish of Moyne – Templetouhy: The Story of a Tipperary Parish*, I could imagine the hours, days and years which have been expended on its creation. The work was initiated by the Parish Historical Group in 1990, and initially George Cunningham worked for several years with the group, directing the work and giving it its fine structure. In 1999, William took over this task. There were up to forty local people involved in assembling the material, and William worked on it for four years. He pays a warm and well deserved tribute to all of the people involved, and points out that the work is happily now available for study or research and will be into the future.

William later became associated with Art Kavanagh and he co-authored *Tipperary Gentry, Vol I* about five families of the Premier County. This fine work was published in 2003.

Latterly he has completed a major body of work on the history of the Irish Farmers Association. Joe Rea from Cahir, who was a very popular and hardworking President of the IFA, suggested that this work could bear the name *Knocknagow To Brussels: Origins and Achievements of South Tipperary IFA 2001-2005*. This title referred to Charles Kickham's book, *Knocknagow* and to the small tenant farmers of his time, and also to the progression onward to the founding of the NFA, later to become the IFA. William also made warm mention of the great work so successfully undertaken by T. J. Maher from Boherlahan, a man of vision, tenacity and strength of purpose.

More recently *The Keeffes of the Jockey* has come to fruition due to a request by Kevin O'Daly, son of the late Hannah O'Keeffe, who wanted a history of his mother's family written for the extended family. 250 copies were printed and distributed, and William laughs as he reminds me that Jack Lynch, Cork stalwart hurler and later Taoiseach, would often sing *The Banks of my own Lovely Lee* after a successful day on the hurling field at Thurles. He would relax and sing at O'Keeffe's of Horse and Jockey while on a break to shorten the long journey back to the city by the Lee.

As I admired all these wonderful publications and marvelled at the enthusiasm, industry and creativity of my host, I pondered on the great good fortune of the people of Tipperary to have in their midst a man of the character and dynamism of William Hayes of Roscrea.

Peter Meskell, Marlfield, Clonmel, Co Tipperary

CD No. 31
Time: 69.32
Date Recorded: September 2005

One fine afternoon, in the autumn of 2005, I waited at the old church at Ardmayle to keep an appointment with historian Peter Meskell from Clonmel. I had arrived a little early and as I wandered among the weathered gravestones, and felt the soft breath of history all about me, I looked forward to my meeting with a man who had generously agreed to share with me his deep knowledge of this ancient place.

The village of Ardmayle sits beside the River Suir, four miles south of Holy Cross Abbey. When Peter Meskell arrived he first drew my attention to an old Norman tower house, Castlemoyle Castle, which was owned by a branch of the Ormond Butler family in the 1400s, and which is still in a reasonable state of repair.

We made our way into the grounds of the old church, built on the site of the medieval parish church of Ardmayle. I admired the imposing tower, built in the early 13th century, later altered on several occasions and which is all that remains of the original church. The present church was built in 1815 by the Church of Ireland, and had later fallen into disrepair, as it had not been in use regularly since the 1950s. Then, in the late 1970s, there was uproar locally when a plan was devised to demolish the church and use the stone in the restoration of Holy Cross Abbey. The local Catholic parish took over ownership of the church and graveyard, which allowed the Ardmayle

Heritage Society to begin restoration work on the church.

I was very interested in hearing about any evidence of early civilisation in this area and Peter told me that while attending Secondary School in Cashel, his inspiring teacher, Joe Irwin asked the students to go out to their own neighbouring fields to try to find anything of historical or archaeological interest. Two boys went to the Moate at Ardmayle and found a perfectly preserved Stone Age axe head, shaped and polished, made from blackish stone.

There is also firm evidence of Bronze Age habitation here, as confirmed by the discovery of the Ardmayle Hoard, now in the Belfast Museum. It is thought that the Hoard was found in Ardmayle Fort, Fort Edward, which is situated north-east of the church and which has only recently been identified as a Stone or Bronze age burial mound.

The whole area is dotted with ring forts, and Peter pointed out that without excavation it is impossible to pinpoint the relevant dates. The Moate is technically a motte and bailey, built in 1185 and is a well preserved Norman construction. Only one wall remains of a Tudor style manor house at Ardmayle and another castle or tower house was built on the west bank of the River Suir, but has now disappeared.

During the Cromwellian confiscation, existing buildings were put to use by the new settlers and it was not until the 1750s or later that the fine local big houses were built. Peter pointed out that the lovely Longfield House, now owned by the Coolmore Stud empire, is the best local example of such gracious old buildings.

During the period 1550–1650, prior to the coming of Cromwell to Ireland, Castlemoyle Castle was unoccupied and the Ormond Butler family lived in Nodstown, two miles north of Ardmayle. During the late 1500s Theobald Butler, of the House of Dunboyne, known as the Baron of Ardmayle, was a very wealthy landowner, who built a Tudor mansion on the banks of the Suir, and planted extensively around his property. At this time, the population of the village was 300-400 souls, who were self sufficient, and well able to conduct their business affairs locally. The village was a hive of activity, and included within its confines a bakehouse, a couple of blacksmiths, an alehouse, a tailor, a saddler and a number of carpenters and stonemasons.

The landscape looked very different then to that which met our gaze that September evening. There were no ditches or fences, everything was commonage, though there would have been temporary fencing erected around land which was under tillage.

Peter held me spellbound as he spoke of the ancient roadways in the locality, Boherlahan and the Boreen Caol and he also described the Double Ditch, and the tragic story of the massacre at Ardmayle in 1641. History tells us that " a parcel of idle young men of the vulgar sort" raided the property of Mr Kingsmill in Ballyowen near Dualla and ran off his cattle and horses. The idle young men picked a powerful and dangerous victim, as Mr Kingsmill was brother-in-law to William St Ledger, president of Munster and a Cromwellian appointee. He was a vicious individual and no friend to the Irish race. At his command a troop of cavalry, and some militia from Cashel, were sent to sort out the situation. They went on the rampage around the countryside, and one morning in November 1641 they thundered down the steep incline to Ardmayle village. All the men and youths of the village had left to work on the land, and any old man, woman or child who was caught out of doors was slaughtered indiscriminately. Nine people lost their lives and many more were badly wounded on that terrible day.

We pulled our minds back to the present peaceful afternoon as I enquired about fishing on the River Suir. I was told that the Guinness Book of Records relates that the largest salmon ever hooked with a rod and line in the British Isles was that caught by Michael Maher at Ardmayle in 1868.

We walked amongst the ancient headstones in the graveyard and Peter pointed out some stones which had no identifying symbols. These marked the resting places of the very poor, whose families placed a large stone on the grave to mark the site. He spoke of the local stonemasons who decorated the headstones of the more wealthy people, with symbols of their trade, or with symbols of the Passion of Christ, and he also related the story of the symbol of the cock in the pot, sometimes found on Irish gravestones.

We remembered the Cillíns, as Peter described an old burial ground, situated about two miles south of Ardmayle, which was obliterated almost 15 years ago, and had been in use until 1920. This was a place where stillborn or unbaptised infants were buried, usually at night by the father of the deceased child.

We made our way inside the church, admiring on the way the plaque erected to commemorate the founding of the Ardmayle Heritage Society. In the vestry Peter laughed as he told me that the architect who worked on building the church in 1815 sent his bill to the Select Vestry on regular occasions over the following twenty years, but to no avail. It was decided after two decades had passed, at an emergency meeting of the Select Vestry, that as nobody now on the Vestry Committee had ordered the work to be done, they could not be held accountable for the money due. That was the end of that!

We admired the old fireplace in the vestry, which is still in working order and which has an extraordinary flue, 40 feet in length, running along the side of the church.

The Grubb family are commemorated at Ardmayle Church by four memorials, which had to be removed from the walls during the recent restoration work, but which were

The Ormond Butler Towerhouse, Castlemayle Castle, built in 15th Century.

replaced later at the request of the family. Peter told me that the Grubbs were flour and corn millers in Clonmel, who left the area in the 1920s. A descendant, Louis Grubb, is responsible today for the mouth-watering Cashel Blue Cheese, which is highly acclaimed both in Ireland and abroad.

William Carson, MD was appointed rector of Ardmayle in 1868 and worked here till the late 1880s. He had previously run a lucrative practice as a surgeon and had been a late vocation. He was uncle to Lord Edward Carson, who spent many happy summers living at the rectory at Ardmayle. Later in his career it is recorded that Edward would declare that he had spent "the happiest days of his life riding an ass around Ardmayle." He was introduced to hurling by the local lads, and would later organise a hurling team at Trinity College in Dublin. He was the first person to commit a set of hurling rules to paper.

I listened enthralled as Peter described the hurling teams of earlier days, when the game was supported enthusiastically by the landlords and matches were organised between the various estates. There is a fine record of hurling games being played in Tipperary long before the founding of the GAA and I was intrigued to learn that cricket was also a popular rural sport. This game was played in spring and early summer, when a smaller area would suffice, as all the larger fields, necessary for hurling, were then under meadow.

"The hay is saved and Cork bet" is a saying I've always associated with a year's work well done, but Peter explained that it had a different meaning entirely. Until the hay was saved there was no large field available to train a team, or indeed to play a winning match against Cork or any other great hurling county.

I heard about the day-long hurling tournaments of the 1880s and 1890s, conducted as part of a carnival event which included athletics and football tournaments as well as hurling, and attracted hawkers, storytellers and singers by the score.

The glorious game of hurling was discussed between us, and the vexed question of whether or not skill with the sliotar and camán was passed down through families was teased out. Peter recalled a book he has written on a local team, 'Suir View', which represented Tipperary in the Inter-county Championships in the 1890s. It was very noticeable during his research that these giants on the hurling field were followed in due course by their descendants onto the great hurling teams of later generations.

Time was moving on, but there were many more subjects I wanted to discuss with Peter Meskell, as I was enjoying his great company and was reluctant to leave him. He very kindly agreed to meet me again, and accompany me on my wonderful journey of discovery around the lands of sweet Ardmayle.

The restored medieval church at Ardmayle

CD No. 32
Time: 55.50
Date Recorded: September 2005

There is a great Gaelic football tradition alive and well in the Kingdom of Kerry where I live, and indeed my own family has been actively involved in All-Ireland finals for two generations, but it was my father-in-law, Dan O'Hea of Kilbrittain, Co Cork, who first sparked my enthusiasm for the game of hurling. In his younger days he had won many an honour on the hurling field, and the game continued to be a consuming passion all the days of his life.

As I spoke to Peter Meskell in the restored church at Ardmayle, it occurred to me that here was a man ideally placed to fill in the many gaps which still remained in my knowledge of the origins of the game of hurling, so I prompted Peter to give me his views of the subject of inherited skills with the hurley and sliotar. He maintained that competitive spirit is definitely inherited, as is physical and moral courage and the will to win, but the essential ingredient for sporting success is practice, fitness and hard work.

Faction fighting at one time played a major part in the lives of the Irish people, and Peter feels that the earlier forms of hurling and football were closer to faction fighting than they are to the modern games, though it would be entirely wrong to infer that the game of hurling sprang from faction fighting. Records exist which prove that the game was played in Ireland from earliest times, albeit with a hurley of a different shape and a ball of about double the size of the sliotor now in use. There were twenty one players on a team and the earlier game was somewhat similar to the game of hockey as it is played today.

When Peter Meskell was researching his booklet on the "Suir View" team of the 1890s he was lucky enough to trace some sons and daughters of the men on the original team. He was told that in those days the ball was played high and low, with no lifting; 90% of the play was on the ground. 'Scoobing' the ball was a common description of the play. Peter had always thought that this word was a corruption of 'scooping', but was delighted to learn that 'scoobing' came from the Irish word for sweeping – 'ag scuab'.

We had a great discussion on the garb worn by the hurling teams of the 19th century and later. Looking at old photographs of the local teams, it can be seen that the players always wore caps, "like the old time cricket caps" Peter explained. Jerseys which felt like hair shirts were the norm, as were knickerbockers long enough almost to meet the stockings, and light boots, probably with steel studs.

Team jerseys were always worn, and Peter pointed out that the present team jersey was not unlike that worn by the Tubberadora team of more than 100 years ago, which was black in colour with a yellow sash.

Reluctantly, we dragged our minds away from the glories of hurling and made our way into the tower, the oldest part of the church at Ardmayle, which survives since the 1200s. Peter explained that the early church towers could be defensive if the church came under attack, and he pointed out the embrasure in the wall, which had plenty of working space on the inside, and room for a musket to be fired through the opening. From the outside the target was very small and was defensively very efficient. We climbed the staircase, which had been fitted during the restoration in the 1980s, and reached the first floor. This was probably used from 1815 onwards when the church was rebuilt, as a meeting room, or for the storage of records. Up on the second floor, I admired the chimney breast which had been so unobtrusively set into the stonework as to be virtually unnoticeable. As we climbed to the top floor, the great bronze bell, fitted in 1815, came into view and as Peter struck it and the fine clear tone rang out over the village and countryside, the sense of history and endurance was palpable in this ancient place.

As we enjoyed the birdseye view of the graveyard below Peter explained that the original church, built in the 13th century, would have been longer and wider than the present building. It would have resembled an English Norman parish church, where the tower would be an appendage to the church, whereas now the present church seems to sit as an appendage to the original tower. The roof of the tower would have been of a pyramid type, which would have been visible from outside. When the tower was being repaired during the building of the present church in 1815, it is felt that some cutstone was taken from the nearby Tower House, as a great variety of such stone is visible today, built into the tower.

I was keen to know how the actual restoration work of the 1980s had come about. The Heritage Society set about raising funds initially, once the parish had been assured that there would be no added burden on the parish funds, and work began as part of a Fás Youth Training programme. The work on the fabric of the tower was not a huge drain on resources, but to fund the overall work on the church, card drives, dances and table quizzes were initiated and the people of the parish proved more than generous. Peter made special mention of T. J. Maher, who was then MEP for Munster, and who was successful in getting two grants from the European Union to help with the restoration. There were up to 40 young local people working on the church, employed by Fás, many of whom have gone on to work very successfully in the trades learnt on the training programme.

Before we left the tower, we stopped to take a close look at two early headstones which had been removed from the graveyard for safekeeping. One of the stones is most beautifully and delicately engraved, and another has been identified as a medieval grave slab, dating from 1200-1500 AD.

Viewed from the outside the dimensions of the original church are clearly envisioned when one stands at the north wall, and looks at the remains of the foundations. The original church would have been in excess of one and a half times the length of the present church, and four to six feet wider. It is easy to imagine how the church would have stood in relation to the tower, which would have looked more like a belfry in those earlier days.

We discussed the origins of the Parish Historical Journal, as Peter told me that some years ago, he had written a history of the Parish of Boherlahan-Dualla. Though this was a substantial publication, he found himself frustrated by having to edit and curtail his material – he felt he could not give his subject justice. He approached historian

Tom Ryan and his sister Marion to discuss his predicament, and once the seed was sown for the undertaking, the 'usual suspects' were rounded up and officers and committee were appointed to get the Journal on its way. I was very pleased to hear that great work is now being done on researching the history of local fields.

I had heard on my travels around the locality that the Whiteboys had been very active hereabouts, and when I mentioned this to Peter he smiled and said he had a story to tell me. The extraordinary aspect of this story lies in the fact that it has been handed down to him from the lips of his grandmother, who was born in 1897. She had heard it from her own grandmother, whose grandmother, in her turn, had borne witness to some of the events which occurred on Christmas Eve 1804.

A group of Whiteboys in the area decided to raid the home of Mr Fawcett of Clonoulty, in their search for arms. The landowner was away for Christmas and had left his property in the care of an employee named Gorman, who was also a member of the Whiteboys. He was unaware of the plot hatched by his comrades, and because of his sense of duty and loyalty to his employer, he refused entry to the house by the Whiteboys. They tried unsuccessfully to smash their way in and Gorman fired a shot at random through the fanlight over the door. One of the Whiteboys, named Buckley, was shot in the lung and was carried away across the river by his comrades. He was placed temporarily in a brake of bushes for safety, while a door, for use as a stretcher, was procured from a local house.

Later that morning, when Peter Meskell's great great grandmother, then aged 7 years, was walking to Mass on Christmas morning with her mother, they met some women who had walked past Aughnageeragh Ford on their way to Mass and had heard moaning coming from the bushes there. Taking fright, they scattered and ran on their way, but after Mass, having gained some courage and curiosity, they checked the bushes at the Fort on their way home. They found nothing there. The injured man had died during their absence and had been taken away and buried at Ardmayle.

Richard Long, local Magistrate and landowner, got word of the shooting at Clonoulty and was determined to track down the Whiteboys. On hearing of the burial at Ardmayle he ordered that the body be exhumed so that it could be identified, and known associates arrested. Some of Long's servants heard of this and alerted the Whiteboys, who immediately took the body and reburied it at Clonoulty. Long once again was informed of this development and ordered that the body be exhumed, and once again the gruesome reburial was undertaken by the Whiteboys. This task was repeated for several months, until finally the body found rest at Ballysheehan graveyard, where it lies to this day.

This story prompted a discussion on more recent states of conflict, and Peter had a most interesting theory to explain the lack of any real involvement by members of the local youth in events during the dark days of the War of Independence and Civil War. He told me that during these years, the Boherlahan team was right in the middle of the greatest hurling period they had ever enjoyed. During a 15 year span, they won 9 or 10 county championships and, as was possible in that era, they won two All-Ireland finals. The comradeship and the hurling were never so good, and the game was so time consuming that the young men were already striving towards a cause, and needed no other. Dualla, on the other hand, which had a much weaker hurling team became a hotbed of activity in those turbulent days of war, and while listening to Peter explain his theory, I could not but see the logic and credibility of his words. "The hands around here were busier than the hands in Dualla," he laughed, bringing to mind the old saying "The devil finds work for idle hands."

I shook hands with Peter Meskell as the evening drew in and we turned our backs on the church at Ardmayle. As I faced my car towards Kerry and home, I reflected on the fact that we are fortunate as a nation to have, in every part of Ireland, people such as Peter Meskell, who will so ably and so willingly push open the portals to the past, and allow us to enter, to listen and to learn.

The late Michael Hassett, Birdhill, Co Tipperary

CD No. 33
Time: 59.15
Date Recorded: February 2004

In the year 1775, Patrick Hassett and his young family were evicted from their home at Quin, Co Clare. With his wife and four children he walked for five days across the Clare hills until they crossed the Shannon at Killaloe. He was then given a mud hut for his family by the local landlord at Knockadrummond near Ballina, where he eked out an existence for many years. This story of courage and endurance was related to me by Mike Hassett, a direct descendant of Patrick Hassett, when we met at his home outside Birdhill one chilly day in February 2004. Since that day, Mike has tragically passed away, but when we met he was in great form and he very courteously invited me to accompany him on a tour of the locality.

As we rambled along our first stop was at the site of the old school at Cooleen. The land for the school was donated by the local landlord, after the famine in the 1840s, and the teacher, who came from Ballina, was paid by voluntary subscriptions alone. The school on this spot survived, and education continued, until 1895.

As we walked, Mike pointed out an area where stone was cut and dressed in the 19th century. The place was owned by the Lynch family and much of the stone was used in the building of railway bridges during the 1840s.

We came to the spot where Mike could obviously see in memory, a long old house which had belonged to the O'Haras. Not a sign of the building remains today but the family is remembered very kindly. Tom O'Hara was a weaver, "weaving for all Co Clare". He used lambswool from Clare which he spun into thread to make yarn, which he then sold at 4d per yard. His brother had a lime kiln, and when the lambswool arrived from Clare, the vehicle was reloaded with lime for the return journey across the Shannon.

We continued on our way till we came to the "new" road, built in 1800. Locally this is called the 'Canada Road' as it was designed by an engineer who came from Canada to undertake the project. Eighteen families were evicted by the landlord Mr Going, to enable the road to be built, all of whom then had to find shelter in mud huts at the edge of the bog. Families of McNamaras, Hamiltons and O'Haras were among them, and the last of these families left the bog only thirty years ago.

As we approached the site of an old school and orphanage, built in the 1820s, Mike related a most interesting story about the place. Protestant and Catholic children were taught here initially. The Protestant bible, the "Cat Breac" which had been translated into Irish by the Bishop of Meath, was used for religious instruction. When the parish priest discovered this, he ordered that all the Catholic children be withdrawn from the school. Later on in the decade, the old school was revived and Catholics were once again educated there, but no religious instruction was included in the day's work. Mike Hassett's grandfather attended school here for a short time.

From this spot, we had a commanding view of the Clare hills, and the islands on the Shannon. The Banna Islands are, interestingly, part of Co Clare, and are the only lands in Co Clare which are included in the Diocese of Cashel. "And still they gazed and still the wonder grew" I mused as Mike and I talked of the two creameries which operated in this area in bygone days, and the valuable old steam driven pump used by the creamery, the only one of its kind in the world. This is made of solid brass and still sits 60 feet underground. Mike assures me that it will still survive intact a thousand years hence.

We continued on our ramble and stopped to view the ruins of a gracious old house, which was burnt in the 1920s. This was the home of the Twiss family, built in 1862. It was a great pity to burn the beautiful house, Mike felt, as the Twiss family were good people who had had the Black and Tans moved out of the place a short time earlier. Only ivy covered ruins stand sentinel here today.

Mike related a tragic story about thirteen children who died of fever within hours in a local orphanage in the 1870s, and who are all buried in a mass grave at Kilnastulla Graveyard. We stood here at the tomb of Fr O'Brien, who was chaplain to Louis XV, and who escaped during the French Revolution and returned to Ireland, his health in ruins. He died within a year of his homecoming. A Protestant church was built here in 1790 and Mike felt that this was probably the oldest parish in Ireland. Also in this graveyard, lies the last of the Going landlords. His grave stands isolated from all the other resting places and the markings on the gravestone have become illegible over time. Graves of the White family, renowned historians, also lie here, as do those of the O'Brien family of Limerick.

As we reversed our steps back to the comfort of the Hassett home, Mike pointed out The Little Cave – Cooleen – in the slight fall of a nearby field. This was the site of an O'Brien mansion, taken over by Cromwell's man Lieutenant William Sheldon, who, fearing for his safety, left for Nenagh not long afterwards. It was later occupied by the Hastings family.

Ahead of us stood a mighty rock, standing alone in a field, and Mike assured me that a lot of folklore is attributed to its origins. There is a story of Oisin who buried his trumpet here, of the wonder dog Bran, who was killed by a bird, and several other legends of old are attributed to the site.

In a field named Riasc, there stands on a height a great ring fort and Mike maintained that the area was once very wet. Up to about six hundred years ago, the field would have been under water and dominated by the fort, standing proudly above, and visible for miles around.

The February day had grown chilly, so we were happy to arrive at the family house once more, to sit at the old range in warmth and comfort. Once we were settled, the discussion turned to events of the more recent past. "There was a right tough crowd knocking around in my young days" said Mike as he recalled the Broy Harriers, who harassed the people for information about the local Blueshirts. He told me about a big Blueshirt meeting in Nenagh, and about a local teacher who, on qualification, was unable to get work due to his background in the Blueshirts, and who left to fight in the Spanish Civil war. This man had a miraculous escape during that war, when several of his comrades, whom had had just left, were killed when they walked on a landmine.

We journeyed back in time once again to the mid 19th century, to the time when George Twiss became the local landlord in 1840. "The names of the townlands were all wiped out in Twiss's time" said Mike. I wondered aloud about the reason for this, and was told that an old man had assured Mike, about 40 years ago, that the idea was that if a person was brought up in Court for an offence and was asked his name and address, it could be argued by the defence that no such place existed.

We talked of local villages and their names, and Mike agreed with me that the village of O'Brien's Bridge is a really beautiful place. The first 14 arch bridge was built here in the 17th century, and rebuilt with only eleven arches at the end of the 18th century.

An ancestor of Mike Hassett was taken in chains to Liverpool, for transportation to Melbourne, following a faction fight at O'Brien's Bridge in 1836. In Melbourne, he was released after five days in jail, to work as a carpenter in the city for twelve years. His only payment was two meals a day, and when he gained his freedom eventually, he had no money to enable him to return to Ireland. He saw out his last days in Australia, never to see his homeplace again.

Mike now produced from among his great store of historical papers, a wonderful old photograph of the Twiss house, showing a lady in Victorian costume standing on the lawn with her dog, enjoying the sunshine. He also produced a most detailed genealogy of the Twiss family beginning in the 1700s. He also had in his possession the family trees of the Hastings and Atkins families, part of which he had acquired from the O'Grady family and some information had came from a member of the Atkins family in Australia. The need to establish our human roots is evident from the fact that Mr Atkins, from Australia, has come to Ireland nine times in the past eleven years, in order to establish the details of his family history in Kerry and Tipperary. On the day I sat with Mike Hassett in Birdhill, he was looking forward to the next visit of Mr Atkins, as he felt he had been "put astray elsewhere" during his quest, and Mike had some vital information which would put him back on the right path.

Sadly, not long after our day together, this gentle and knowledgeable man was to die tragically, but his enthusiasm, knowledge, humour and generosity of spirit have stayed with me as I remember, with great kindness my good friend Mike Hassett.

The Twiss House, Birhill built in 1862 by George Twiss, burnt 1921.

Paddy O'Dwyer, Thurlesbeg, Cashel, Co Tipperary

CD No. 34

Time: 45.21

Date Recorded: September 2005

The study of local history is a passion in the life of Paddy O'Dwyer and I felt privileged to be invited into his home at Thurlesbeg one late summer evening, to discuss the origins of this great passion, and the hugely important documents he has traced through his fascinating researches.

Paddy has been teaching history ever since he completed his training as a secondary school teacher. His career began at St Joseph's in Dublin, where he taught for two years, followed by a number of years at CBS in Cashel and more recently at Cashel Community School, where he has taught for twelve years.

I was interested to hear about the sources Paddy O'Dwyer uses when researching local history, and his eyes lit up as he described his first bit 'find'. In 1975 he attended a conference on local studies and he seized the opportunity to enquire, from one of the speakers from the National Archives, if information existed about the Blue Coat Hospital, now known as the Kings Hospital, in Palmerstown, Dublin. He was told that in Palmerstown there exists an archive of old records, and immediately Paddy made an appointment to view the archive. A mine of information awaited his attention.

About a mile from Thurlesbeg, lies the townland of Nodstown which covers about one thousand acres. In 1675 Kings Hospital, a Protestant school for wayward children in Dublin, was bequeathed this property which was to be run for the benefit and upkeep of the hospital. In the archives in Dublin, Paddy found a treasure trove of letters, written to Kings Hospital, during the years 1862 and 1863 by the tenant farmers on the estate in Nodstown. The letters relate to the minor famine in the area, the extremes of weather, and include urgent requests for abatement of rent. The tenants at that time had decided to write directly to the hospital rather than use the agent as intermediary.

Paddy read each and every letter and has no question in his mind about the importance of the historical detail each contains. There is valuable information here on the prevailing conditions, on the amount of rents due on various properties and on the amount of reduction in rent for which each tenant appealed. The family names included are invaluable source material for the tracing of family history. The letters may be studied at the archives of the Kings Hospital in Palmerstown, subject to prior appointment, and the information contained in the letters, together with that in Griffith's Valuation for the 1850s, provides a vital link to earlier days in Nodstown and its vicinity.

An interesting fact was clarified for Paddy by reading the information in the letters. Contrary to his earlier belief that the landlords in those days were the instigators of most of the evictions of tenant farmers, "there was more to it" he told me. He explained that after the famine many people left for America and a better life, as they saw no future for them in Ireland. Among the letters there was a call from the local agent in Cashel to Kings Hospital, appealing to the trustees to wait a little longer for the rent, as he was alarmed at the number of people leaving the estate, and feared that he would be left with insufficient labour to work the land.

According to the census of 1841 there were 531 people living on the estate and ten years later, the figure had dropped to 332 – a drop of 35%. Over the next 30 to 40 years, the numbers declined, as small tenant farmers with very little acreage found it increasingly difficult to survive, and so sold their interest to larger farmers.

During the 1840s the small tenant farmers relied hugely on the potato crop to feed the family and also to feed the pigs and hens. When the potato crop failed only the bigger farmers, who also grew barley and wheat and had access to labour, survived and persisted. Most of the houses on the estate were thatched, up to living memory, and Paddy maintains that the tenants got little financial assistance to slate their houses, unlike those on the neighbouring estate, owned by Charles Bianconi.

I had to agree with Paddy when he said that we all grew up with the belief that after the famine, land grabbing became a common practice, but he explained that his research has shown clearly that this was not the case on the Kings Hospital estate. Many of the smaller tenant farmers were more than willing to sell their interest to more prosperous individuals, as the inadequate size of their holding made it virtually impossible to survive.

I am always interested in local field names and Paddy told me that some interesting information has come to light during the ongoing research by the members of the Boherlahan – Dualla Historical Journal. In Thurlesbeg there is a field which has been known historically as 'the famine field'. The wall separating this field from its neighbours is totally out of character with the general banks and hedgerows of the surrounding acres. The cut stones in the wall are two foot long and one foot high and wide, and it is felt that the building of the wall was undertaken as Famine Relief work, and that the cut stone was taken from a nearby castle.

In the year 1869 in the townland of Marshalstown, 5,000 people assembled for a Tenant League meeting on the estate of the Smith-Barry family. The present owner of the land is a descendant of the Chairman of that meeting and one of his fields is known to this day as the 'meeting field'. A fascinating article on this link with our history can be seen in the issue of the Boherlahan-Dualla Historical Journal for 2000.

We talked of other field names and of Mass paths, and Paddy says that he can recall people journeying on their way to Cashel and using the fields as a 'right of way' to which nobody objected. We talked of butter making and its importance, which reminded Paddy of the story of an unfortunate lady who married into a house locally. Her mother had to come to help her to make the butter as her own butter making became something of a liability to the economic welfare of her new family!

A woman's dowry was of the utmost importance in earlier days in Ireland and it is recorded that one hundred and thirty years ago, a local woman married into a farm of 50 acres, bringing with her a dowry of £225 – over 6 times the annual rent. This was the exception, as in most cases, parents scrimped and saved to provide a secure future in marriage for their daughters.

Paddy's granduncle, Con Hennessy was something of a matchmaker, and Paddy's own grandparents' marriage was arranged, and was very happy.

We now returned to the fascinating subject of Paddy's research into the Kings Hospital Estate. He explained that often the agent, who lived in Cashel, came under intense pressure from the trustees of Kings Hospital during the period after the famine, in the matter of unpaid rents. During these years, there were two or three evictions, but unlike our image of scenes of violence and distress, the tenants were 'pushed out gently' here and the goodwill of the farm would be bought thus giving the tenants the means to emigrate. When the estate rents were not being satisfactorily paid, Kings Hospital would send representatives from Dublin to do a survey of the estate, which in time worked to the benefit of the tenants.

As in all areas of Ireland during troubled times, leaders of men quickly became evident, and one such person was local man Michael Ryan Wall, who lived at Castlemoyle. He was the main organiser of the Land League Movement and was on the Board of Guardians in Cashel. His hard and valuable work was rewarded by several months in jail, as the system of boycotting began to have an effect on some landowners. In 1880 a local man, who owned 300 acres, was barred from driving his horse and car into the church grounds on Sunday morning for Mass, as he had traditionally been allowed to do. He had refused to support the Land League, and the people who barred his way that Sunday ended up in court and were fined one shilling for their audacity.

Parnell's *No Rent Manifesto* was recalled as Paddy told me about the terrifying consequences endured by one farmer who decided to pay his rent. The story goes that his child was lucky to escape with its life when shots were fired into the family home on Christmas Eve 1881.

I marvelled at Paddy O'Dwyer's energy, commitment and enthusiasm for local history, as he described the summers he has spent researching in Dublin and elsewhere. The animation evident on his face was a joy to behold as he outlined the three days he spent recently in the National Library. He was searching for vital information, without any success, until finally on the third evening important and substantial data fell into his hands. As he described the scene, I began to understand the thrill and excitement he feels when the pieces of the jigsaw fall into place, and the portals to our historical past are pushed just marginally more wide.

Sister Placida Barry, Ardmayle, Co Tipperary

CD No. 35
Time: 47.28
Date Recorded: November 2005

In November 2005, on the occasion of the launch of the Tipperary Collection of recordings in the Irish Life and Lore series at Mount St Joseph Abbey in Roscrea, Sr Placida Barry stood up to recite the words of the old song *Sweet Ardmayle*. Nobody in the room that afternoon could have been in any doubt about her deep and abiding love and respect for her native place and its people.

The previous month I had met with Sr Placida in Nenagh and she generously agreed to recall for me her early days at Ardmayle, her vocation to the religious life, and her full and varied career working on the missions with the Presentation Sisters.

'Mel' Barry was born in 1940 in Ardmayle, into a most industrious and gifted family. She has one brother Mick, and her father worked in the Grubbs estate. Her mother was an instructor in craftsmanship, most particularly basket weaving for which she was very highly regarded.

Sr Placida explained the origins of the name 'Ardmayle' which means 'high bald hill'. The village lies in a dip between two hills, and while it is sometimes said that the bald hill refers to Prices Hill, she feels that it is more likely that it is the Moate which gives the place its name.

When Charles Bianconi, the Italian peddler of songs, sat on the moate at Ardmayle to rest, and spied the glorious Longfield House across the Suir, he made a resolution that one day he would be rich and would become the proud owner of that lovely place. This came to pass following the great success of his coaching business in the early 1800s and he was to become a great and a generous benefactor in the area.

During Sr Placida's childhood, Longfield House was occupied by Molly O'Connell Watson, who was a descendant of the Liberator, Daniel O'Connell, and a lady who is remembered with great fondness in the area. Before she died in England, she specified in her will that her wish was to be buried in riding gear and brought to her burial place in a horse-drawn carriage. Each of these wishes were complied with, with the co-operation and support of her neighbours in South Tipperary.

Sr Placida's maternal grandmother was a member of the Huguenot family of Ferncombes who had left France due to persecution after Louis XIV withdrew the protection they had enjoyed under the Edict of Nantes. The family settled in South Tipperary in the parish of Clonoulty, and brought with them to Ireland their exquisite skills of craftsmanship. Sr Placida's mother inherited those skills, and as a child Placida recalls bringing tea to the family at the river where, waist deep in water, they harvested the rushes for the basket weaving. The rushes were tied together for ease of carriage, and brought home to the farmyard. When they had dried to a golden brown colour, they were ready for the weaver's expert touch. Placida's mother was an instructor in crafts with the ICA and was instrumental in setting up a co-op with other local craftworkers, who brought their wares to a shop in Dublin to be sold. She died in 1994, having worked at her beloved crafts right up to the end.

I enquired of Placida if she and her brother had also become absorbed in craftwork and she said that indirectly they had helped, in that they freed their mother to create her lovely pieces by helping with the household tasks, which were many and varied due, in part, to the absence of electricity. The gift of craftsmanship has indeed been passed down, as Placida demonstrates. She describes her love of gardening and flower arranging and her brother Mick's skills at crafts, which have also been inherited by his children.

The decade of the 1940s in Ardmayle was vividly brought to life as Placida recalled her early days in primary school there. Each Tuesday and Thursday afternoon, the butter making days, children would gather outside the creamery window to wait for Tom Murphy to hand out a mug of buttermilk to be shared among them, to ease the weariness of the long day's learning. The Master of the school was James O'Brien, and conditions in the school were extremely basic. Turf was brought for the fire each day, as was spring water which was collected by the boys, and kept in the classroom in a bucket along with a mug for dipping and drinking. Master O'Brien always wore a hat, which he would place on top of the wardrobe, beside the fire, when lessons were about to begin. When he donned the hat again it was time for play, so out everybody would troop, to be supervised at play by the mistress. The hat would then reappear on the wardrobe, visible through the window, where it would rest until it was time to return to work, and once the headgear disappeared from the wardrobe playtime would be over once more. The children at Ardmayle School were 'world travellers' as each day a child had some story to tell about an event in the outside world. The class would gather around the map of the world which hung on the classroom wall, find the relevant place, and listen as the story unfolded.

Sr Placida feels very strongly about the closeness and supportiveness of the local community of her youth, and right up to the present time. She spoke to me of the response of neighbours when a family was in trouble, "everybody held them" she said, and they were lucky to exist in an "area of caring, conversation and content." She spoke of funerals, of the harvest and the meitheal, and declared that many a good match was made at a threshing, as the dancing went on long into the night. The Tubberadora hurling team was given proud mention and the respect shown to people of all religions and beliefs and for different faiths was recalled. She remembered one Protestant gentleman who learned the Rosary so that he could pray respectfully and meaningfully at the funerals of his Catholic neighbours.

Continuing the story of her schooldays, Sr Placida recalled that when she reached the appropriate age to begin secondary school, a High Nellie bicycle, with a good carrier for her books, was bought for the daily journey to Cashel to the Presentation Sisters. She made many friends there, and the Sisters spoke openly to the girls about their community and their working lives. In 1955 the Presentation Sisters from Castleconnell, who were involved with missionary work, came to Cashel to speak to the girls about their work and this sparked a determination to serve in the young girl from Ardmayle. Her parents, once they had recovered from their initial shock, were very supportive, and they were to say in later life that their daughter had always been closer to them than she could ever have been as a married woman.

In 1960, having taken her vows, Sr Placida went to study at UCC, and she told me a fascinating story about an occasion when her brother collected her in his car from UCC to bring her back to Castleconnell. He diverted to Ardmayle, where all the neighbours had gathered in the home farmyard to greet her, but due to the strict religious rules at that time, she was unable to enter her home, and met her family and neighbours at another local house.

The late Hannah Barry admires her wonderful work

She left Ireland to work on the missions, having completed her studies at UCC and she had no hesitation in declaring that if she had the chance, she would live the same life over again. She loved working in the developing world and felt privileged to be involved in the work of these very challenging and far-flung arenas.

We returned in memory to Ardmayle as Sr Placida related a story concerning her father, to illustrate for me the absence of a dividing line between the natural and supernatural worlds in earlier days. Mr Barry was walking up the long avenue of Longfield House one moonlit night, when he felt he was joined by an old friend, Dan McGrath, who silently walked beside him, and placed a hand on his shoulder. Mr Barry knew at that moment that his old friend had passed out of this world, and that he was happy and at peace. He was always afterwards convinced that this was an authentic experience and an unremarkable event in his life, related to the supernatural world.

We spoke of the banshee, of pisheogs, of Holy Water and its importance, and Placida smiled as she said "in a farmer's house, there might be a gun in the rafters, but there was always Holy Water by the door." She treasures the fountain pen her father gave her on entering the religious life, and recalled the Rosary beads she was later to present to him to fulfil her side of the bargain!

Though life has taken Sr Placida to places exotic, strange and impoverished, she says she delights in "slotting back in" when she goes home to Boherlahan, to the friends and neighbours she has known all her days. She marvels at the fact that the young educated people of today would regard her earlier memories of her home place as similar to tales of centuries ago. While she agrees that life has moved at an extraordinary pace in the last 60 years, she feels that the young people of today are standing on firm foundation stones set down by the strong, true and enduring people of earlier times.

Before I took my leave of Sr Placida I asked her to recite for me again the lovely evocative old words of *Sweet Ardmayle* and she concluded our most enjoyable few hours of conversation by reciting a modern tribute to the schoolhouse in Ardmayle, written by Molly Ryan.

I could have happily stayed and listened to Sr Placida's recollections for several more hours, but the modern world with all its intrusions came calling and we both had to respond, having promised that we would meet again before many months had passed.

Bill Collins, Coolboreen, Newport, Co Tipperary

CD No. 36
Time: 38.59
Date Recorded: January 2004

When I began my work of collecting the oral tradition of Tipperary, I was very conscious of the fact that that some of the old songs and ballads of the county should be included. On a raw January afternoon in 2004 I arrived at the home of Bill Collins at Coolboreen, outside Newport, and was welcomed inside the house by the man himself. Bill is a man who has a fine repertoire of long local ballads which have survived down through the years, and as soon as he began to sing I knew I had struck gold! The voice was sweet and true, and words concise and descriptive, and I happily sat back and prepared to be entertained.

"The Bullock Fair Day"

On 23rd October, both simple and sober
I went down to Newport to sell an old cow,
T'was a fair of renown that was held in the town,
Called the Bullock Fair Day sure everyone know.

Oh! The morning being still sure I felt rather ill

Sure myself and my comrade went into John Ryan's
Who kept a nice shop with a beautiful drop
Like the dew on the mountain it sparkles and shines.

We had two pints of stout sure 'twas then we walked out
Sure we said 'twas too early to take anymore
For fear we'd run tight and get drunk before night
That happened to many in Newport before.

It was just half past 8 when I thought 'twould come wet
Such numbers of people I ne'er saw before
They were there from Murroe, Ballina, Killaloe,
Castleconnell, Birdhill and likewise Cappamore.

There was carloads of girls with fringes and curls
Bags stuffed with hay as they sat at their ease
But when they got down and moved through the town
Their white stockings were splattered with dirt to their knees

It was then half past 10 when they all crowded in
There was woeful confusion all over the town
The pigs they were squalling and the cattle were bawling
The horses with wagons they drove up and down.

There was humour and pleasure and courting at leisure
Whiskey and porter was flying and much more
Each man with his lover sure he went into cover
And the steam from the punch came out from each door.

From drinking the whiskey sure they all get so frisky
In each public house there was nothing but rows
Sure they whacked it like blazes from Corbett's to Hayses's
The ladies Caplices, Butlers and Cowens.

There was pegging with bottles and choking of throttles
Bricks stones and bottles were flying like the rain
Till the police hauled them and quickly installed them
Gave them peaceable lodgings that night in the jail.

I said I'd go home sure twas time for me come
Twas a wonder the old cow didn't ramble away
Sure the prices was bad, sure I should bring her back
And long I'll remember the Bullock Fair Day.

Bill and I had a good long laugh about the antics at the fairs of long ago. "Sure they were always fighting at fairs" he said, implying that it was as much a part of the day's business as the haggling and the hand spitting and the honest financial dealings.

"Did you ever hear the song *Martin Gleeson's Ass* Bill enquired, and before I could answer he was away, in fine voice.

Oh ye all knew Martin Gleeson
He was a regular tip-top swell,
He lived down in a nice slate house
Longside Cragg Blessed Well.

Times were getting very bad
He had run scarce of grass,
So the only thing he had to do
Was to play cards for his ass.

They were there from Castleconnell
And from Newport town so fair
From Galway, Cork and Kerry
And from every part of Clare.

They were driving out from Limerick
Since after second Mass
In motor cars and carriages
To play for Gleeson's ass.

I'll give ye the donkey's history
Before ye play a card
He was always quiet and honest
He never did blackguard.

But he had one little failing
Not a public house he'd pass
And if you didn't tie him up
He ate the people going to Mass.

Several verses followed describing the music and the fare on offer, the mutton, beef and ham, cheese, bread and jam, lots of Murphy's Porter and bottles of Bass. In the heel of the hunt, poor Martin Gleeson lost his ass to Mickey Carty from Lisnagry, and so the ballad concludes:

I had pity for old Martin
He began to weep and wail
He went out to bid his ass goodbye
He kissed his head and tail.

He threatened Mickey Carty
To feed him well with oats and grass
And that ends the daily dango
Playing for Martin Gleeson's ass.

The narrative in the ballads is so descriptive and humorous, and it is obvious that Bill Collins enjoys every word he sings. He seemed to be watching the scene in his mind as the song unfolded. I asked how he could remember all the verses and he assured me that if he heard a song sung twice, it remained within him. We spoke of the dances of long ago in the Newport area, and recalled three wonderful musicians, Mrs Connors, Mrs McGrath and Mrs Ryan Bán, all concertina players who were "out and out music to the world. You'd hear nothing like it now. They were brilliant."

It was time for another song and this time the ballad told a tragic story of an event which occurred during the occupation of Ireland by the Black and Tan forces in November 1920.

The Bridge at Killaloe

The news had spread from Ireland
And it rang from shore to shore
Of such a deed no living man
Had ever heard before

Not even those in Cromwell's time
Would do the deeds they do
In the way they murdered those poor youths
On the bridge at Killaloe

Three of the four were on the run
They were searched for all around
Until the hero Egan
Was found in Tralee town
And when at night while in their beds
Were captured while asleep
The way that they ill-treated them
Would cause you blood to creep.

They tied them up both hands and feet
With ties they couldn't break
They took them down to Killaloe
With steamer on the lake
Without sentence judge or jury
Like dogs they shot them down
And their blood flowed with the Shannon
Convenient to the town.

Some descriptive verses follow which detail the funerals which saw "100 clergy all robed out in white" and then concludes with this verse –

The 30th November boys
In history will go down
They were sold and traced through Galway
And found in Tralee town
But the day will come when all will know
Who sold their lives away
Young Roberts and McDermott,
Brave Egan and O'Shea.

This stirring historical ballad, detailing a dreadful event in the early part of the 20th century brought a powerful image to mind and caused me to reflect on the awesome power of words to convey real horror, grief and tragedy.

Bill now lifted his voice in song once again and the sweet and romantic words of the old song *Mary from Murroe* filled the room. This prompted a discussion on matchmaking and its merits in past times, and led on to talk of hard times financially, of emigration, of farming traditions, of local creameries and of schooling. Bill recalled two wonderful teachers who taught in Newport before his time. These men were named Fitzgibbon and O'Donoghue, and they are remembered with gratitude down through the generations in the town.

A song about Ireland was next in Bill's repertoire, and a beautiful old ballad it was, full of feeling and nostalgia. The final verse went –

> I love every blade of green grass on your mountains
> Every leaf on your tree, every rock on your strand
> I love your green hills and your murmuring fountains
> And I love you forever, my own native land.

I felt I could sit forever with Bill Collins, and listen quietly to his sweet and tuneful songs, but the January evening was darkening, and I had many miles to travel, so reluctantly I prepared to take my leave. As I did Bill began to hum to himself a vaguely familiar air, and he smiled at me as he named it *Tipperary Far Away.* The penultimate verse begins –

> I remember 1930, we won the Triple Crown,
> We sailed the briny ocean, to play on Polo grounds
> Came back the world champions, proudly for to say
> We are the conquerors of Tipperary.
> Tipperary far away.

> So now we'll all return home
> To the slopes around Slievenamon
> Where the men of old in days of yore
> Did pike and make the hay
> With the maidens there with their dark brown hair
> We'll sing and dance all day
> In magnificent Tipperary,
> Tipperary far away.

Pakie Ryan, Tullow, Newport, Co Tipperary

CD No. 37
Time: 62.96
Date Recorded: September 2005

In Tullow, Newport, Co Tipperary lives a man by the name of Pakie Ryan, and a well renowned man he is, as I discovered on my quest for the oral history and tradition of the county of Tipperary. His name was mentioned to me on several occasions before I had the pleasure of meeting him at his home, one fine evening in September 2005.

As we settled ourselves comfortably, I enquired about the meaning of place name of "Tullow" and was told that most people translate the word to mean a mound or a hill, but the original Gaelic element of the word suggests a coming together for a contest or comórtas.

There are Neolithic and prehistoric sites in this area, but the original settlement is the early Christian ring fort. Pakie described this as a single ring fort of 50 – 60 metres in diameter, set on high ground, providing a good aspect overlooking the Mulkear valley. Along by the river there exist prehistoric millsites, and also more recent examples which date from the mid 19th century.

Pakie Ryan has a good, hearty chuckle and he gave me a fine display of this as he mused that the area was not terribly important archaeologically, but concedes that he will probably get into all sorts of trouble for this blasphemy, adding that he is, after all, a blow-in!

There is a wide variation in the quality of the land in this area, from the flood plains of the Shannon to the west, to the top of Keeper Hill, at over 2500 feet high. Newport itself was a planned settlement, and Pakie pointed out that many of the river names of Ireland also date from pre-Celtic times.

Veterinary surgeon Pakie Ryan came to Newport in 1968 from his previous home 25 miles away. He laughs as he tells me that he settled in the real stronghold of the Ryans and recalled a team in which he played in his younger days which boasted thirteen Ryans among the players.

We decided to take a stroll outside and the surrounding lush farmland brought to mind the placenames and fieldnames to be found in all rural areas of Ireland. This is also true of the Tullow area, and Pakie told me that the name of the local river can change as it flows from one area to the next. We talked of the excellent drainage work which has been undertaken over the years, and I was reminded that the word 'hinch' as it appears in placenames, refers to a place which is flooded in winter and which dries out in summer.

Newport was built on the confluence of three townlands at a crossing point on the river. The Earl of Roden, who was born north of London, came to Dublin in the early 1700s to study law. He was to make a fortune at his profession and later become Chancellor of the Exchequer. He acquired huge tracks of land in various areas around Tipperary including Newport, where he built the Charter School. His sister married a member of the Waller family of Castlewaller, Newport, and Pakie told me that in all his time here he has never known a local person to refer to the townland as Castlewaller – it is always known as 'Cully', a derivative of the Irish word 'Coilte', meaning wooded area.

The later Wallers have a somewhat poor reputation locally, something that Pakie feels may be a little harsh. In earlier generations the family got the charter to hold the fair at Newport in the 1750s, and they subsidised tolls to encourage the sale of cattle in the town and their subsequent export from Limerick port. Records from that time show that at the October Fair held on 23rd October, 10,000 to 15,000 cattle would be sold, and in the Scully diaries it is recorded that Mr Scully bought 300 cattle at Newport on one occasion, suggesting that the amazingly high number of sales recorded may indeed be credible.

Old placenames mentioned to me were Fair Hill, now known as The Square in Newport, and the road which leads to the Ryan property is known as Custom Gap Road and has been since the 1850s.

We spoke of the Hedge Schools, of the Charter School established in Newport in the 1750s and of Fr Cook, the first post-Reformation priest to be made Parish Priest of Newport in 1795. He had been head of a prestigious college in Paris, and being privately wealthy, he funded the first church in Newport, which shares with Cashel the distinction of being the first two post-Reformation churches in Cashel and Emly. In 1790 a very able Protestant clergyman, Canon Pennyfeather, had built a rectory at Newport and carried out further work on the church and Pakie feels that Fr Cook was sent to Newport so that "one good man could mark another".

We had a fascinating discussion on Mass Rocks, on Cromwell's practice of persecuting all sects and not alone the Catholics, his stabling of his horses in cathedrals in England just as in Ireland, and the suggestion that he was equally active against the Church of England as he was against the Church of Rome.

The influence of the Vikings in Ireland was immense, as has always been recognised and Pakie told me that recent DNA studies prove that Irish blood has a major element of Viking content. The studies prove that the Vikings who came to the North of England, Scotland and Northern Ireland originated from the region of Finland, and those who made their way to more southern regions originated from Holland and the Low Countries. Thus it can be said that the Normans who came to Ireland were of the same stock as the Vikings who had settled in Brittany in France, and who 200 years later made the precarious sea journey to our coast. The Normans settled and assimilated well in Ireland and an important point made by Pakie Ryan is that they began to pay wages to their Irish labourers, unlike the Irish chieftains who had offered protection, but no wages up until that time.

There is little Norman influence in the area around Newport, as the land was not suitable for tillage. I was told about John Lackland, son of Henry II who came to Ireland in 1185 with three important friends, Theobald Walter, William de Burgo and

Philip of Worcester. The families of the Burkes and the Butlers were recalled and the connection with Abington Monastery was explained. The terrible days of the Penal Laws were remembered as Pakie explained that many of the middle class farmers in Tipperary at that time held onto their lands due to the great influence of the Butlers in those perilous days.

The sun was sailing westward beyond the hills of Clare, gilding the lowlands and the waters of the mighty Shannon river as we made our way indoors once again, I listened enthralled as Pakie talked about his own life as a veterinary surgeon. His father had always worked with animals and was well renowned as a very good cattle doctor. Pakie qualified in 1968, having spent the previous five years studying. He spoke with admiration of Canon Hayes of Muintir na Tire, who, having read about the testing for tuberculosis in cattle in Britain, persuaded some local farmers to test their herds voluntarily. The practice was later to be officially undertaken by the Department of Agriculture in the 1960s and was compulsory from then onwards.

Pakie Ryan is very happy with his life as a vet, a profession which he says keeps him in touch with all levels of society, keeps him informed about place names, boundaries and townlands, and feeds his great passion for history and for heritage.

Tadgh Pey, Ballindown, Birr, Co Offaly

CD No. 38
Time: 57.43
Date Recorded: February 2004

On a darkening February evening, with the wind from the east, and a sickly low sun playing hide and seek through banks of cloud, there is nothing more likely to warm the heart than the blaze of a good turf fire and the warmth of excellent company.

Both of these gifts were mine on an evening in 2004 when I met Tadgh Pey at his home in Ballindown. Tadgh has an immense knowledge of the early history of his native place, and I began our conversation by asking him about the legend attached to the nearby Rath of Moylena. He spoke of Conn of the Hundred Battles, High King of Ireland in the 3rd century AD, and of Eoghan Mór, King of Munster, and of the jealousy between them which led to a battle at the Rath of Moylena. Conn's army occupied the fort, and planned a surprise night attack on the army from Munster. The Connaught Fianna refused to fight during the hours of darkness, and Conn's forces were thus depleted. The Munster men were gaining the upper hand in the battle until the sun rose over the Slieve Blooms, which allowed the Connaught Fianna to enter the fray and the tide of battle was turned. Eoghan Mór, King of Munster, was put to death by the High King of Ireland and the men of Munster were put to flight. There were to be two more major battles at the site in the following centuries. "The Commandos of today would run for their lives" declared Tadgh, if they were confronted by the Fianna of old.

The ruling class then held sway in Ireland and the Brehan Laws were enforced and obeyed by the princely, noble and bondsmen classes, while the Druids, or holy men, inspired the spiritual lives of the people. St Patrick was later to absorb the Druidic beliefs into the Christian beliefs, and Tadgh's theory is that the blessed wells and sacred bushes of the Druids were blessed by Patrick and thus became Christian symbols. A few of the Druidic customs still survive and I was fascinated to discover that in one local area, nobody would ever strike a beast with an elder rod, as the elder was the sacred bush of the Druids. This respect for the elder bush could be described as "a fossil memory" according to Tadgh.

There were seven Holy Wells and a Mass Rock at Cloughal and at Tober na Pearla, - the Well of the Pearls, where tiny marbles could be seen which had been washed up from underground and left lying in the bottom of the well by the retreating water. About 50 years ago, the wells were obliterated as a result of a reclamation plan, but the Mass Rock survives, surrounded by a quarry. Happily the owner of the quarry has guaranteed that it will be allowed to stand in its ancient place without disturbance.

Tadgh Pey chuckles as he responds to my query about ghosts and fairies which may have populated the area, or the imagination, in other days. He maintains that most of the stories one heard were probably made up to frighten the listener. One instance he recalls happened at a house on the Ridge Road, almost a mile from his home. The ruin of an old farmhouse was said to be inhabited by fairies, who would throw children up to the rafters and catch them on the way down. There was also a story about fairies joyriding on a cart causing the jennet to be unable to pull it. The Parish Priest of Banagher went to bless the place with holy water, and as he began his work, a little man appeared and began to argue with him, whereupon the priest hit him between the eyes with the holy water. The little man told him he'd have to come back a second time to the place, which he did, whereupon the fairies took their leave, never more to return.

When Tadgh was growing up in his ancestral home, which he still occupies, "popes, princes and potentates" were discussed and analysed nightly by the neighbours who would call. Many tall tales were told along with more truthful ones. As a child he would sit and listen to stories about the hurling matches played all night by the fairies in the ring fort, until at dawn, when the cock crowed, play would be abandoned. He listened in awe as he was told of the ragworth, an buachalán búi which could be turned into a fairy horse by the fairies and galloped away.

Tadgh is convinced that he has a rational explanation for the dreaded crying of the banshee, which was regularly heard in Ireland on the death of a local person. In the month of October the cry of the vixen sounds like an unearthly wailing which "would curdle your blood" and this sound, he feels, is the origin of the funereal ologóning of the dreaded banshee.

I was keen to discover the names of the prominent families in the area historically and Tadgh named the O'Carrolls as a major force. Very few of the O'Carroll chieftains died in their beds and factions of the family were continually fighting. There was mention of the daughter of Garret Mór, Earl of Kildare, who married an O'Carroll, of Silken Thomas, of Ely O'Carroll, of Fear gan Ainm, of the Butler Earls of Ormond, and of Charles O'Carroll, who in 1598 held a feast following his victory at a battle with the Butlers. He had employed eighty McMahon gallowglasses from Monaghan and rather than pay them their dues, he plied them with drink and slaughtered them all. Hugh O'Neill, Earl of Tyrone, and patron of the McMahons, took his revenge by driving out all the O'Carroll cattle and burning their crops.

Coming closer to the present day I wondered if poaching had been a local pastime in the area, and Tadgh told me that his uncle, Bill Pey, had been caught poaching at the Earl of Rosse's estate, but prior to his imprisonment had escaped to America. The local young lads loved poaching and "tormenting the Earl", but Tadgh feels that perhaps the Earl was quite happy to see them escape censure and go off to America "out of the way". A local man named Jack Hernon had been caught poaching in Lord Rosse's preserves and escaped to New York. He later sent home a ballad he had written about the joys of his pleasurable activities around his native home. It was a pleasure to listen to Tadgh recite the words of the old ballad, and the real feeling expressed through Jack Hernon's words was so evident and so vital.

Tadgh Pey has always loved the land, the ploughing and the tractor work, and has lived a happy and contented life as a bachelor farmer. The house he occupies was first leased from the Rosse estate in 1828 by his great grandfather, and will be passed on to his niece, so that the Pey family name will persist on this spot. His father was involved in the Land League, and boycotting and cattle driving were practised in the area. One man who had leased a grass farm for eleven months for grazing had his 200 cattle driven off the fields and back to his yard. Twelve men from the Ballindown area were imprisoned for twelve months in Tullamore jail as a result. "There was more bitterness about land than about politics" Tadgh told me, as the people depended on the land for their livelihood and were expected to pay high rents for land which they considered to be their own.

Rath of Moylena, Ballindown townland near Birr.

Bog butter found in Deinagh Bog, Now in the National Museum.

The area was not too badly affected by the Famine of the 1840s, though many people set sail on the famine ships in search of a better life. In the nearby townland of Ballinagulsha, which is on the edge of the Esker, a population of 60 families was recorded in Griffiths Valuation of 1854. The family names included Kellys, Butlers, Morisseys, Fletchers, Clarkes and Birds. Today only one family remains.

On my travels in the area, I had heard a mention of "The Phantom Thresher" and I asked Tadgh to tell me of this strange and tragic occurrence. In the autumn of 1946, a spailpín fánach, a travelling farm labourer, came to work in the area. He was an innocent and hardworking man, whose sole and oft-proclaimed ambition was to win the big prize of £30,000 in the Irish Sweepstakes, which he would use to buy a tractor and threshing mill. One eventful day a telegram was delivered proclaiming him the winner and he immediately sent off his order for the machinery. Shortly afterwards it became clear that the telegram had been a cruel hoax and the unfortunate farm labourer was found hanging from the rafters, to the horror and dismay of the local people.

The autumn of that year was stricken by terribly wet weather, which resulted in great worry for the safety of the harvest. At a farm near Lackaroe, two men were digging potatoes, and watching for the threshing machine which was due to arrive from Kinnity. Eventually, they saw the machine on the road, so they left their potato digging and went down to meet it, only to find nothing there at all. Some three hours later the actual mill arrived at the farm and panic ensured when it could not be manoeuvred into the haggard. Eventually, fearful of some supernatural cause, the farmer sent for the local curate, Fr Martin Ryan, who blessed the machine, which eventually got through the gap, and the threshing proceeded without further incident. It was felt in the locality that the first thresher spotted on the road was a phantom machine related to the tragic events of the previous months. A letter written by a lady who said she spotted a canvas covered travellers' caravan coming up the same road at the time of the sighting of the first threshing mill never convinced the local people that this may have been what the two potato diggers saw that autumn day sixty years ago. This story with many others is told in detail in Tadgh Pey's book "Where the Beautiful Rivers Flow" which was published in 2005.

Darkness had fallen, and the wind had picked up as I took my leave of Tadgh Pey's home at Ballindown, but the warmth of the fire, and the warmth of his welcome enfolded me on my long journey south westwards to my home in The Kingdom.

The Pey home built in the late 1600's.

The late Jack Ryan

CD No. 39
Time: 62.21
Date Recorded: September 2005

One summer's day in 1940 photographer Father Frank Browne SJ, was passing through Leighlinbridge in Co Carlow, when he spotted a young girl of perhaps six years of age, filling a bucket of water at the pump at her home. He photographed the occasion and the charming result can be seen in the book "Fr. Browne's Ireland" above the caption 'Swinging on the pump at Leighlinbridge (1940)'.

Sixty five years later, at the home of Maura O'Brien at Dualla, I was to meet Breda Tierney, the young girl at the pump in Fr Browne's photograph. She remembers the occasion well, and the fact that she was not tall enough to reach the handle, and had to jump up and down with the handle to get the water to flow. She recalled that one of her sisters would later insist that it was she, rather than Breda, who featured in the photograph, but Breda is insistent on the point. Her mother was later to sew a ribbon onto the pink dress in the photograph in order to lengthen it, and Breda refused to wear the garment again. There is no ribbon visible in the image, so Breda was indeed the water carrier that day in 1940.

The pump is still in its position in the old place, home to Breda's family which comprised of six girls and one boy. One sister, Mary, was also photographed by Fr Browne in 1940 and this sweet image captioned 'Girl and Gramophone' was featured in the 1999 Ark Life Calendar. Breda laughed as she recalled that Mary was very musically talented, and a lovely singer. She was allowed "skive away from work" to go to listen to records on the gramophone with the priest's housekeeper, who was her music teacher. They were photographed with a little dog, and the gramophone, in the local convent garden in the summer of 1940 by Fr Browne.

Two historical photographs came to light during my conversation with Breda, both of which feature her father, Colonel Jack O'Farrell. The first was taken on the occasion of the opening of Aras an Uachtarán, and the second at Islandbridge, as Oliver St John Gogarty released two swans into the Liffey in the company of W. T. Cosgrave, President of the Irish Executive, Mrs Cosgrave, W. B. Yeats and Colonel O'Farrell who was acting as the President's ADC at that time. Earlier, Jack O'Farrell had worked as an undercover agent with Michael Collins. He accompanied Collins, to London for the signing of the Treaty in 1921 and would have been in Beal na Blath on August 22nd 1922 to witness the tragic events, if his orders had not been changed shortly beforehand.

Breda Tierney's schooling was completed at St Leo's, Carlow, and after her Leaving Certificate she decided to train as a nurse in England. Following a brief period nursing in Mount Carmel Nursing Home in Dublin, she made the decision to join the army, on the advice of her cousin who was an Army Chaplain in Korea.

She was based initially in Catterick, and then spent three great years in Gibraltar where she met Winston Churchill, Aristotle Onassis and Maria Callas, during various cocktail parties. Onassis, she recalled, was very astute "with a brain like a scissors" and the gorgeous black dress and glittering diamonds worn by Callas remain vivid in Breda's memory.

She made several visits to Spain during her term of duty in Gibraltar and was later transferred to Germany to serve at the BAOR Headquarters as Captain. Nicosia, in Cyprus, was her next posting, during the Suez Crisis. The situation there was dangerous and volatile and at one stage, the city was out of bounds for about a month. The nurses and midwives spent many of their off duty hours working on embroidery, and, as the threads had run out, Breda and a friend decided they would take a chance and go to the city to replenish the supply. While making their purchases shots rang out and Breda saw a man fall at her feet, and another some few yards away. Once it was obvious that medical assistance was available, the two nurses, with their precious threads, beat a hasty retreat back to base.

Breda later spent tours of duty in Singapore, Malaya, Hong Kong and Nepal, and during her six weeks annual holidays she would go to Calcutta, on unpaid leave, to work with Mother Teresa. She remembers the saintly nun with great kindness, and admired her businesslike approach to each and every problem.

Picture of Breda Tierney's sister Mary with her music teacher, 1940.
(Photograph taken by Fr. F. Browne - © Fr. Francis Browne SJ Collection)

Oliver St. John Gogarty (second left) releases two swans into the Liffey at Islandbridge as
President W.T. Cosgrave, Mrs. Gogarty, W.B. Yeats and Colonel J. O'Farrell (Mr.
Cosgrave's ADC) look on.

I was filled with admiration for Breda, as she explained the dire conditions under which she worked voluntarily in Calcutta and Darjeeling during her holidays in those days, and she told me that, as a family, she and her siblings had been reared to be unselfish and caring, and that subsequently she had always been thus, "the same two and fourpence", in her own words..

On one of her trips home from Hong Kong, Breda was to meet her future husband, Billy, on the plane, where they became acquainted initially. Once home, she was to stay with her sister in Greystones, and on her arrival there, her sister and brother-in-law were preparing to go out to a party. Though exhausted from travelling, and reluctant to socialise, Breda eventually agreed to accompany them, and one of the first people she met on arrival at the party was her travelling companion from the plane.

Not long afterwards Billy and Breda decided to marry and Breda was then to be kept busy caring for her mother-in-law and uncle, who were unwell for many years. Latterly she had been caring for her husband until his death, so she was being very truthful when she told me that she has spent much of her eventful and fruitful life caring for people.

Maura O'Brien, in whose home we were recording, had sat enthralled through all of Breda's reminiscences, and I now noticed that she had in her hand some lined pages upon which notes and lists of names were written. She told me that the notes had been kept by her late uncle Jack Ryan, who was a member of the Dualla branch of the Volunteers in the early days of the 20th century. Here was some very interesting historical hand-written material relating to local Volunteer activities during the years 1914-1922. The entry for 1914 reads –

"National Volunteers. Bandoliers, haversacks, belts, dummy guns. August split after letter was read by Pierce McCan that an attempt was being made in Dublin to hand over the Volunteers to the Government. A new Coy formed under the leadership of Pierce McCan, now called the Irish Volunteers, looked upon with suspicion by the enemy 'G' men."

The ninetieth anniversary of the 1916 Rising was just months away as I read those words, so I quickly turned the pages till I came upon the entries for that tumultuous year.

"Coy fully armed, all parades dogged by enemy servants. Coy target practice. Miniature rifle armaments consisted of shot guns (single bore) £1 each. Mairtini Henery rifles. Service rifles, some short arms and home filled shot gun ammunition. Literature – weekly issues of 'The Volunteer' and current Sinn Féin publications. Armed public parade to Mass in Dualla 17-3-16. Weekly drill at Ballyowen. Easter week Coy under arms in Ballyowen Ho. Guard withdrawn by order. Arrest of McCan. Enemy cavalry and 'G' men. Volunteers'

homes visited by R.I.C and searched for arms. Some arms taken. Some given up, and some retained. Release of McCan. August. Reception from Goolds Cross. A temporary lull in public volunteer activity and dispersal of Coy as existed heretofore. Important dispatch riding to Fethard. Plebicite put in storage after dismiss."

Also listed are the names of the Dualla Coy. Irish Volunteers 1916.

Pierce McCan	Anthony MCan	Tommy Walsh
Jack Walsh	Laurence Grant	Patrick Grant
Owen Keevan	Ned Moloughney	Pake Kerwick
Thomas O'Brien	Tommy Dwyer	Dick Power
James Dalgan	Jack Gorman	Willie Gorman
Jack Looby	James Looby	Paddy Looby
Jack Murphy	Thade Ryan	Patrick Mulcahy
Joseph Mulcahy	Paul Mulcahy	James Ryan
Jack Ryan	Tom Treasy	Jack Skehan
James Hennessy	Patrick O'Donnell	Patrick Casey
Patrick Horgan	Patrick Kerwick	Timothy O'Dwyer
James Grant		

There are sixty nine names on the list for 'D Coy. 3rd Tipp Bde. I.R.A', names such as Treacy, Grant, Keevan, Dwyer, O'Donnell, Nolan, Mulcahy, Skehan, McCormack, Nagle, Barrett, Ryan, Breen, Dargan, Flanagan, Delaney, Barnable, Wardyke, Loughlan, Fitzgerald, Walsh, Gleeson, Murphy, Carroll, Looby, Lawrence, O'Grady, Sullivan, Shanahan, Hennessy, Burke, McGuire, Grace, Lacy, Cleary, Kennedy and Hogan.

Maura O'Brien has a very clear memory of being brought by her uncle to Pierce McCan's house in Ballyowen. In the garden there stood an old tree, and her uncle related the story about McCan, who hid in the tree to escape capture by the military, but was given away by his dog which had followed him to the tree and stood whimpering on the ground below. Her uncle Jack broke a branch from the tree as a memento, and Maura took it home to her parents for safe keeping.

We retraced our steps in time, as Breda joined again in the conversation to speak of her father who was a most generous man in his dealings with those less fortunate. Her grandmother would provide milk and yellow meal in a big pot for impoverished children going to and coming from school, and sometimes potato soup and scraps of meat were also provided for the hungry scholars.

"There was an unmerciful row in the morning" laughs Breda as she begins to relate a story of one Christmas morning in her early childhood. Her dearest wish was to be given a yoyo as a gift from Santy, though she assured me that she was at that time of an age not to believe in the great man. Very early on Christmas morning, she crept downstairs and with lighted matches checked all the presents that Santy had brought, and laid along the top of the piano in the parlour. Each present had the name of its recipient written on it. Breda decided that she would "re-arrange the whole issue" by changing all the names to different presents, so that she would get the skipping rope intended for her sister. Breda laughed so much at the memory and at the dramatic consequences that we had to pause in our conversation and laugh along with her until she got her breath back.

Maura was reminded of a memory of her own when she recalled that Santy left her a note one Christmas morning, regarding the necessity to eat more so that she would grow big enough to ride a bicycle. Her persistent enquiries of her mother as to the similarity of her handwriting to that of the man from the North Pole were never fully answered. She recalled two posters, drawn by Brian O'Higgins which were displayed each Christmas in her home. One wished *Happy Christmas from Big Christmas morning to Little Christmas night, May every heart be filled with joy, gladness and delight.* The second had less to say, simply wishing everybody a *Happy New Year.*

There was talk of the turnip being brought in at Christmas and decorated with holly and silver paper to hold the red Christmas candle, of the turkey, the goose and the cured ham, the party pieces recited and sung, the community spirit alive and well with neighbours being invited in for the entertainment, the Wren Boys with their whistles, melodeons and fiddles, and as one memory prompted another I almost felt that I too had been present in those earlier days in Tipperary, participating merrily in the fun and the laughter.

That autumn evening in Dualla had sped by as I listened to the recollections of two fine ladies who have lived such generous and fulfilled lives both at home and in far flung lands, and the warmth of their company and the sound of their laughter remained with me long after I took my leave and began my journey home.

1916 — 500 yds 3.3 1000 yds No 3

Coy fully armed. all parades dogged by enemy servants.
Coy target practice. miniature rifle armaments
consisted of shot guns (single bore) f each. Mautini
Henery rifles. Service rifles. some short arms
and home filled shot gun ammunition.
Literature – weekly issues of "The Volunteer"
and current Sinn Fein publications. Armed
Public Parade to Mass in Dualla 17-3-16
weekly drill at Ballyowen. Easter week.
Coy under arms in Ballyowen Ho. Guard
withdrawn by order. arrest of McCan.
enemy cavalry & 'g'men. volunteer's homes
visited by R.I.C. and searched for arms.
some arms taken. some given up. and some
retained release of McCan August.
reception from Goolds cross. a temporary
lull in public volunteer activity and
dispersal of Coy as existed heartofore.
important dispatch riding to Fethard. Plebicite.
put in storage after dismiss.

Page from Volunteer Jack Ryan's notebook, relating to local events in 1916.

Dualla Coy Irish Volunteers. 1916.

Pierce McCan	Thade Ryan
Anthony McCan	Patrick Mulcahy
Tommy Walsh.	Joseph Mulcahy.
Jack Walsh.	Paul Mulcahy.
Laurence Grant	James Ryan
Patrick Grant	Jack Ryan
Owen Keevan	Tom Treasy
Ned Moloughney,	Jack Skehan
Pake Kenrick.	James Hennessey.
Thomas O'Brien.	Patrick O'Donnell.
Tommy Durye	Patrick Casey.
Dick Power	
James Dalgan.	
Jack Gorman	Patrick Hogan
Willie Gorman.	
Jack Looby	Patrick Hackett
James Looby.	Timothy O'Dwyer.
Paddy Looby.	James Grant
Jack Murphy	

Page from Volunteer Jack Ryan's notebook listing the
Dualla Company Irish Volunteers 1916

D Coy. 3rd Batt. 3rd Tipp Bde. I.R.A.

Paul Mulcahy.	Tom Treacy	Wm Carroll	Jack Burke
Joe "	Jim Grant	Jim Dwyer	Jack (Dagan) Burke
Pat "	Larry "	Jack Walsh	Bob McGuire
Wm "	O'Keevan	Billy Breen	Jim Ryan
Con Dwyer.	Jim Dwyer	Tom "	Tom Grace
Jack Skehan.	Eddie O'Donnell	Jerry Nolan	Ned "
Tom McCormack.	Paddy Nolan	Jack Looby	Jack Lacy
Tom Nagle.	Jack Wardyke	Jim "	Jim Cleary
Jim Barrett	Mick "	Lawrence "	Jack Kennedy
Martin Ryan	Paddy Loughlan	Tom Lawrence	Jim Murphy
Phil Breen	Eddie Fitzgerald	Andy O'Grady	Jim Barago
Dick "	Tommy Walsh	Paddy "	Paddy Hogan.
Jack "	Andy Gleeson	Denis Sullivan	
Dick Dagan	Jack Murphy	Tom "	
Joe Flanagan	Ned Ryan	Gerald Ryan	
Jack "	Thade "	Bill Shanahan	
Jack Ryan	Bill "	Tom "	
Wm Delaney	Jim "	Jim Dwyer	
Jack Barnable	Dick Walsh	Jim Hennessy	

Page from Volunteer Jack Ryan's notebook listing the names of D Company 3rd Battalion 3rd Tipperary Brigade IRA.

Michael Joy, Portroe, Co Tipperary

CD No. 40
Time: 41.21
Date Recorded: September 2005

One chilly autumn day in 2005, I climbed with Michael Joy to Townlough Upper, in the parish of Portroe, and stood to gaze in wonder at the famine ridges laid out before us. Potatoes had been sown here during the 1840s, but the ridges had never been dug as the people had died of starvation or famine fever or had boarded the famine ships. The ridges stood before us in stark reminder of cruel and desperate times in the Ireland of the 19th century.

Michael Joy is a local historian, and it was my very good fortune to spend some hours with this most knowledgeable of men at his beloved homeplace. As we recalled the famine in the area Michael told me that there had been a soup kitchen about half a mile away, but as it was situated on a height, many people died whilst climbing uphill in an attempt to reach it.

We travelled a little further to see the graves of the Leinstermen, where the King of Leinster is buried in view of his beloved kingdom, in accordance with his last wish. Brian Ború, High King of Ireland, married a sister of the King of Leinster in about the year 1000AD. The King of Leinster was obliged to come to pay tribute to the High

King, but on his arrival, Brian Ború was up in Clare taking care of some urgent business. The High King's wife mocked her brother for attempting to pay tribute to her husband and the Leinsterman left a high dudgeon. The High King followed him, and a skirmish broke out, and as the King of Leinster was put to the sword, his dying wish was that he would be buried in view of his kingdom. From this spot the Kinnity Hills of the Kingdom of Leinster can be seen in the far distance. The burial ground here dates from pre-historic times, and existed long before Brian Ború took the life of his brother-in-law and had him buried in this ancient place.

From where we stood at Townlough Upper we had a wonderful view of Lough Derg, looking rather grim on this autumn day, and the feeble sunshine on the Round Tower at Holy Island drew the eye to that quiet place of pilgrimage. The counties of Galway and Clare looked glorious in the autumn light. "A scatter of people from various counties" worked in the slate quarries, Michael told me, as we made our way to view the remains of the quarry here. During the famine times, there were 700 people working at the quarries, and their payment was made in Indian meal. The earliest mention of the slate quarries in the area is in Arthur Young's *Tour of Ireland* in 1777. He travelled up to Derrycastle, from where the slate was taken by boat on the Shannon, leaving from Killaloe, and thus the slate became known as Killaloe Slate. A slate quarry at Derrycastle is shown on the Taylor and Skinner Map of 1778, but it is not shown in the Civil Survey of 1654.

Quarrying created great employment in this area, though the work was hard and very dangerous. The owners were the Smithwick family, and the business was run by managers, who were unable to keep the quarries in operation during the First World War. John Bernard O'Driscoll from West Cork got the work underway once more in 1923 and created employment here until 1956.

During the 19th century there was heavy traffic on the Shannon, due to the shipment of slate, almost all of it carried by water due to the treacherous state of the roads. Originally the slate left from Derrycastle, and later from 1826, from Garrykennedy. Much of it made its way up the canals to Dublin, but due to the high transport costs, on its arrival in Dublin the Tipperary slate was more expensive than Welsh slate – a real economic headache for the business people of the Premier County.

The quarry at Townlough Upper was worked until 1932. It was a comparatively small quarry and the men worked with picks, shovels and crowbars. As we entered through the narrow passageway, I gazed in wonder at the sight that met my eyes. The sheer walls

Famine potato ridges at Townlough Upper.

Frolic Bridge at Garrbeg Quarry

are still to be seen, and here stands a lake of bright spring water – a most impressive sight. I asked Michael about the uses to which the slate was put, apart from the roofing of houses, and he told me that the offcuts were used for building walls and fences, and that in local graveyards some beautifully carved headstones can be seen standing proudly in place since the 19th century.

Michael told me that his great interest in local history was engendered by his late mother, who lived until her 95th year. She came from Co Clare and her family name was Quinn. Her father was a carman, or a carter of slate. With a pair of horses, he would transport a ton of slate on a cart with iron shod wheels along very bad roads, for two days and a night, up into Laois and Offaly. Once the slate was delivered to its destination and the journey home had begun, Borrisoleigh was the designated place to rest overnight, before continuing on the long journey home.

As we emerged out of the quarry through the narrow opening, we remarked on our very wet feet. Michael said that "slate stone was always great for water" and that on the journey home from school in his young days, the cold clear water from the wells around the quarry was a real treat on a hot and dusty summer's day.

We made our way gingerly downhill – "mind your ankles" advised Michael – and, in the mist and rain blanketing the lower ground, we came to the entrance to Corbally quarry. This place was worked in the 19th century, mostly by Welshmen, who were excellent slatemakers who used stone to its best advantage. There is a crystal clear lake here which reaches to a depth of 80 – 100 feet. Divers have reported that there lies in the bottom of the lake some old machinery from the quarry, which has lain in the water here for over 100 years.

Michael pointed out the engine house, which had a tunnel to the smoke stack and told me that when slate was delivered to Garrykennedy in the 19th century, coal would be brought back to fuel the engine house. The local men who worked here were often small farmers, who owned a good horse and cart, essential for use in quarry work.

Nothing remains of the old buildings which once stood at this place; the old quarry office, and beside it the RIC barracks, of which there were three in the parish at one time. A certain amount of bickering between the Welsh and Irish was common as they would often "fuel the passions in the few pubs."

A hurling team existed here since the 1880s and a famous match was played against

Ballina, when the local men emerged victorious. In the 1930s and 1940s Michael knew a few of the old men who had played on the team, and he declares that they are still heroes around this place. An old song can be heard proclaiming the might of these hurling men, and Michael recited one verse which lists some of the names which still exist in the parish:

> "Bill Keogh, Martin Minogue,
> Sheridans Jack and Jim
> Pat Molompy and Joe King."

A local tug of war team won all before them in the late 1930s and early 1940s. They were trained by a former PT instructor in the British Army who had married a local girl.

"There's not a stir now" Michael muses, as we stand in this quiet place, and he recalls that there were two pubs and a shop in Corbally up to the days of his youth. Once asbestos slate came onto the market in the 1950s the death knell for the quarries was sounded and in 1956 the Corbally quarry closed, with the loss of employment for the workforce of about 150 men.

It seemed to me, as we made our way back to Michael's home, that we had been visiting another world, peopled by men who knew toil and hardship, who laboured long hours in difficult and dangerous conditions but who rose to the challenge of their hurling and tug of war matches, played with vigour and enthusiasm on their days of rest.

It was a great privilege for me to be accompanied that September day by Michael Joy, a day that I will remember with great kindness for a very long time to come.

Marjorie Quarton, Nenagh, Co. Tipperary.

CD No. 41
Time: 62.01
Date Recorded: January 2004

In the year 1930, at the family home at Crannagh, near Nenagh, Marjorie Smithwick was born, the treasured only child of her proud parents. The house at Crannagh had stood since 1795 and had been extended several times until the 1860s. Marjorie's father was born in 1878 and had inherited the property from his uncle.

In January 2004 I sat with Marjorie at her home in Nenagh, and she smiled as she recalled her "cosseted and pampered" childhood, being cared for by a loving nanny and by extremely devoted parents. She painted a vivid picture of life in the Big House, where as a child she lived a separate life in the nursery until the age of four or five years. All her meals, except for the occasional lunch, were taken with her nanny in the nursery and she did not receive any formal education in her early years. Nanny occupied a special place in young Marjorie's life, "I loved her dearly and wept buckets when she left." There were no other children in her orbit, and as she was reared among adults, she considered herself an adult at the age of twelve.

As a very young child, her mother had taught her to read and write, and though Marjorie loved to learn, her education was somewhat haphazard. She had had several nursery governesses before the age of eight. Lessons were later taken with a girl from Nenagh who would arrive at Crannagh each morning and leave at 1.00 p.m. When war broke out in 1939, and petrol became very scarce, the lessons ceased, and her parents took on the task of educating their nine year old daughter. Marjorie has a most interesting view on the results of their efforts. "My father brought me up like a Victorian boy and my mother brought me up like an Edwardian girl" she mused and declared that neither upbringing was an ideal preparation for adult life in the mid 20th century.

During those years Marjorie took great delight in being allowed to feed the calves on the farm, and she always had a great love of horses, which was to endure all through her adult life.

When she was sent away to school at 15 years of age, she discovered that her knowledge of current affairs and recent Irish history was seriously deficient as she had had the benefit of her parents' own education only, which had ceased around 1914. One name from Irish history did strike a chord, due to the stories she had been told by the maid at home in Crannagh. Her home had been a safe house for Michael Collins and often, on his trips from Dublin to Cork, he would stay at Crannagh, which was a "tricky business" as the place was deep in de Valera country. One morning Marjorie's grand-uncle Tom arrived at the station in Nenagh to meet Collins off the train in a closed carriage driven by Jamesie, the gardener at Crannagh. Near the gate to the platform stood a mule and a dray loaded with barrels of stout. Suddenly the police arrived in force to the consternation of Tom Smithwick, who feared for the safety of his expected guest. Jamesie quietly dismounted from the carriage, backed the mule until the dray was across the gateway, shot the mule in the head and as it fell, the barrels rolled in all directions. In the noise and confusion Jamesie quietly drove away. Collins emerged safely from the station and was picked up later and brought to the safety of Crannagh. In later years, Marjorie's father would sometimes point out to her messages written on the boards of a timber hut in the garden. The initials M.C. were clearly to be seen on several of the messages and were pointed out to the young child with pride by her father, as being the work of "The Big Fellow".

As a child, Marjorie recalls writing little stories, and had always had a great love of "anything to do with words." Writing was in the family as her mother was a cousin of Edith Somerville of Castletownshend who with Violet Martin wrote The Irish RM, Mount Music, Sweet Cry of Hounds and many other books. Marjorie's mother had signed copies of all her cousin's works and would read to her young impressionable daughter from these, and from the works of other famous novelists. Marjorie, though keen to write, was somewhat "scared off" by all these writers, and also by the great journalistic reputation of her Aunt Evelyn, who was the first female correspondent for The Spectator. Many years later, when illness confined her mother to her home, with Marjorie as attendant and carer, the writing gene reasserted itself. A series of articles she wrote on The Farm Dog were accepted by The Farmers Journal and Farmers Monthly and were hugely successful.

She also did a little skit entitled *Shep the Sheepdog Trials* for an English magazine, and this was followed by requests for more about Shep and his adventures. She decided to get twelve of her articles on the farm dog illustrated and printed in Nenagh and has sold 2,000 copies over the years, mostly around her native place.

Later, this work expanded into a book entitled *All About the Working Border Collie* for the All About series. This was in print for over 20 years, until the series was taken over and the rights returned to her, which she in turn sold to an American firm. Subsequently *The Working Border Collie* was published in 1998 and is still in print.

"I had got myself into the kennel" she laughed, as she explained that she had grown tired of writing about working dogs, and so in 1987 *Corporal Jack* was completed and published by Collins Press. This book related to a dog mascot in the Second Battalion Royal Dublin Fusiliers, Marjorie's father's regiment in World War II. Her father had kept diaries during the war and she used the material she found there to illustrate the story of the mascot "Corporal Jack".

Collins Press requested more work, and the resultant book was entitled *No Harp Like My Own*, which took as its theme the consequences of a major trauma on two distinct personalities. This work got very little publicity initially but after two years, due to various factors, it began to take off and has since been a major success.

We took our leave of the world of books and writing, as I felt that the 30 years between Marjorie's early 20s and her 50s must have beheld some fascinating events which we had not probed. How right I was! At the age of 17, when her uncle died, she inherited £100 in cash, with which she bought a horse and 2 bullocks. By the time her father died, when she was aged 26, she had a shifting population of six to eight horses and a dozen cattle, and had paid off half the price of a 13 acre field. Prior to this there had been many days of worry due to the precarious financial position of the family, and Marjorie was in dread that she would have to sell the property on her father's demise. She had had problems dealing with the banks who were unwilling to lend money to a single woman – a fact that still rankles with Marjorie as it would with any woman in her position – so she "put the cheque book in the stove and managed with cash." She built up a very successful business dealing in horses, and running an entirely solo operation.

I was keen to know if at this time she had any interest in marriage and I got a fine chuckle in response to my query. "I was not short of suitors", she smiled, adding that she had been extremely cynical, as she owned 200 acres, and was an only child. She was working very long and hard hours and as a result she was in her 30s when she married John Quarton, who hailed from Yorkshire. They had one daughter, Diana, who now lives in Crannagh with her husband and three children.

Bearing in mind my own background in the antiques business, I listened with interest to Marjorie's stories about her upset in earlier days when, due to her precarious financial situation, she was forced to sell some lovely old pieces of furniture from her old home, and her later satisfaction in becoming involved in the antiques trade herself. Her daughter, Diana, has also inherited the gene, as she bought a shop in Nenagh, and set up and successfully ran "Aladdin's Cave" for many years.

At the age of 68, Marjorie decided the time was opportune to retire from farming, as she had become fed up with the red tape and bureaucracy involved, and had developed a great interest in the work of the National Council for the Blind of Ireland, for which she worked voluntarily. She proudly declares that not many people over 70 begin to earn a salary for the first time, but she was thrilled to do so, as an employee of NCB Ireland. She had always had a horror of becoming dependant, so she decided, at this time, to move into Nenagh from her home five miles away. The old home at Crannagh is now filled with the vibrant young voices of her three grandchildren and their parents.

I am always very interested to hear first hand accounts of happenings of a supernatural nature during far off days, and Marjorie Quarton did not disappoint me, as she related an experience vividly remembered from her earliest days. Her parents always dressed for dinner and often, when they had guests, the ladies would come to the nursery in evening dress to see the little daughter of the house. One evening, as Marjorie drifted off to sleep, she opened her eyes to see a lady bending over her. She was dressed in a gown with a low neckline, framing a cameo broach on a chain, and her black hair was parted in the centre and tied up behind her head. Marjorie closed her eyes, pretending to be asleep as she had always been nervous of the visiting ladies in the nursery, and when she opened her eyes again, the lady had stepped back, and then she was gone. She later asked her mother who her visitor had been, but was told that nobody had been in the house for dinner that evening. "Lady Glorioso" was the name the child had christened her visitor to the nursery. About four years later, while looking through a photograph album with her mother, she spotted the lady with the low necked gown, the cameo and the black hair parted in the centre, "Look, Lady Glorioso" she cried to her mother, who was mystified and explained that the lady in the photograph was, in fact, Great Aunt Charlotte, whose daughter, Emmy, had been born fifty years earlier in the 1880s and had slept in the same room in the nursery as did the young Marjorie.

I listened in fascination to another story about a local boy, who grew up in the hills nearby, and who had an imaginary friend, the subject of much scepticism among the members of his family. The boy grew to adulthood and the friend accompanied him all the days of his life, till at his funeral, a relative, who had arrived late at the graveside, spoke to a weeping man, with long matted hair and beard and the clearest blue eyes. He held a child's rosary in his hands. "I was a friend of his" he murmured through his tears.

The Tale of Gentle Kitty was recounted for me before I took my leave. About 100 years ago, there lived three Maguire brothers in the locality. They were rough and uncouth individuals who were regularly involved in faction fighting. The brothers, all unmarried, lived together, and one of them, known as 'Black Maguire' decided he needed a wife. Every female in the neighbourhood was in fear of him, but he had his eye on one young lady named Kitty. He went to her house where he told her widowed mother "I've come to ask for Kitty". The mother, in terror, attempted to get rid of him, by saying her daughter was already promised. He left, but returned later and to his surprise Kitty agreed to be his wife, as she knew he had land, and she decided she would make the best of things. The wedding was held amidst crying and wailing from the family of the bride, but to the surprise of all concerned, some instinct made her husband kind, and over a period of time she succeeded in civilising him somewhat. One wet, winter day, she ran down the hill to the spring for water, caught cold, and over several days grew progressively more ill, until, to her husband's consternation, she died. Black Maguire became a shadow of a man, who would go about singing the words of a song he had composed for his dead young bride. Marjorie got the words of the song at the age of 12, from a woman who was then aged over 80. People say they still see gentle Kitty running down the hill to the spring, with her hair and her skirts blowing about her, even on the calmest of days.

Marjorie recited the words of the old song *Tale of Gentle Kitty* which the heart broken Black Maguire would sing dolefully, to the tune of *The Gentle Maiden*.

"One year she shared my life and home
And filled my heart with pride,
But at the age of 20 years
My Kitty fell sick and died.
So sadly do I miss her smile
I wish my life away
I called her my Gentle Kitty
and I think of her night and day.

Her face was fair and laughing
Little and sweet was she.
Her heart was kind and tender
As ever a heart need be.
One year she filled my life with joy
Now all is sad and grey.
I called her my Gentle Kitty
And I think of her night and day.

The late Katie Ryan and the late Mary Finn (nee Ryan)

CD No. 42
Time: 57.00
Date Recorded: 1980s

CD No. 44
Time: 42.45
Date Recorded: 1985

CD No. 43
Time: 20.59
Date Recorded: 1985

CD No. 45
Time: 52.44
Date Recorded: 1985

One day about twenty years ago, Maura O'Brien of Dualla decided that she would dearly love to have a recording of the voices of her elderly mother, and her two beloved aunts, who were at that time nearing the end of their days. She had grown up in a family which was very talented in song and recitation, and performances by her elders were a constant source of entertainment during her childhood days. Luckily, she realised the urgency of recording the old songs and recitations before her mother and aunts passed away. We are fortunate indeed that she had that foresight, and we can now be entertained in our turn, by the storytelling, poetry, verse and song of an old family, long rooted in the lands around Cashel.

The voices to be heard in the recordings made at the Ryan family home at Dualla, are those of Maura O'Brien's mother, Ellen (nee Ryan) and her two sisters Mary Finn (nee Ryan) and Katie Ryan, each of whom passed away during the following two years. Maura O'Brien can also be heard. Some friends of the family add their voices during a birthday get together and to the celebration of Mass at the Ryan family home.

When families and friends, who are full of years, gather together, it is inevitable that the discussion swiftly turns to family connections and tracing, and so it was in Dualla in 1985. The Coffeys, Cliffords, Lowrys, Kellys, O'Neills, O'Sheas and Heffernans are all given their turn against a background of the sparking fire in the grate.

"Take a drop of whiskey, go on" instructs one of the hostesses.
"'Twill kill me, give it to me so" comes the reply.
"Good health. I'll have a drop of water in it."
"You'll not get drunk on that anyway" the guest is laughingly reassured.

In a sweet tremulous voice Mary begins to sing *The Harp That Once* and a song is requested from John, who performs *The Sweet Half a Crown,* which tells the tale of a woman who was blessed with many children and was drawing the half crown as a result.

> "Well, myself and my man we're the cocks of the walk
> I've a silver fox fur hanging down
> And no wonder I'm gay on my journey today
> For I'm drawing the sweet half a crown.
>
> And if God feeds the birds with the haws of the trees
> Away with the grimace and frown
> And if all fruit should fail at the end of my days
> I'll remember the sweet half a crown."

A lovely recording can be heard, on the occasion when Mass was celebrated at the Ryan home in Dualla, and the old hymns were sung with gusto, including "Sweet Heart of Jesus", "Soul of my Saviour" and "Hail Queen of Heaven".

Ellen O'Brien, Maura's mother, used to perform her party piece at all the family gatherings, and she can be heard in good voice, telling the story of an old West Cork woman, who, for the first time in her life, struck off on the train for Cork city to sell her eggs. She gets on the train, and is thrilled at the variety of the passing countryside, particularly the telegraph poles, as they rose up and fell back "between the whole lot of them they'd addle you." She arrives in Cork and is amazed to see "ships, boats and motor cars below and beautiful gardens above." Her eggs were successfully sold, and off she goes down Patrick Street, "gawking around." She was in search of a man whom she had known when he was a child growing up in West Cork and who now worked in a gentleman's outfitters in the city, having come up in the world. She located the premises, "a most exquisite house, beautiful with all class of style in it." Her quarry was called onto the shop floor, dressed in a "black suit, with black shoes with painted tops, tails on his coat, a white shirt as thick as anything, and a black bow." "Johnny my darling" said his visitor "sure I knew every bit of you well when you were a garsún, running around through the bogs barefooted, with a creel of turf up on your back. Many's the time when you'd be coming up from the bog, I'd bring you in for a crust and a pinch of sugar on it."

He very quickly ascertained what it was she wanted, "the makings of a couple of shirts", wrapped the parcel, trust it at her refusing payment, and said "do you hear anything? Is it a whistle? It must be the train" and away she flew out the door with her parcel, and off down Patrick Street to the station, much to Johnny's relief.

It is obvious that the old tale, and its telling, gave Ellen O'Brien a lot of pleasure, and as her audience clapped and laughed, it was sad to reflect that three months later, in August 1985, Ellen was to pass away.

"I was driving to the fair in my old side car
When I met with Katie Clare on the road to Castlebar
She was walking I may state, and said I to her 'Oh Kate
Would you like to take a seat in my old side car'

'Oh begor I would' said Kate 'in your old side car
I'd be grateful for the lift as it's miles to Castlebar
And sure if you do not mind and the pony is resigned
I will drive you like the wind in you old side car'

Oh Katie took the reins in my old side car
Sure my hat near burst its reigns on the road to Castlebar
As she drove the little beast, did I mind sure not the least
I was anchored to her waist on my old side car.

Oh an awkward place to kiss is in an old side car

The late Mary Finn prepares for Christmas.

The late Eileen O'Brien (nee Ryan)

> But we tried when she said yes on the road to Castlebar
> Oh then God be with the days when the neighbours all would say
> There goes Mrs Pat O'Shea in her old side car"

The company was treated to this fine old song which triggered another outbreak of tracing, with the O'Sheas, Ryans, Healys, Dillons, Kennedys, Bradys and Walshs all getting honourable mention.

A discussion of pisheógs was next on the agenda, and a local woman who bought a green coat and got it shortened to fit her was recalled. She took the garment home and her mother told her to take the green coat back to the shop or "the next thing you'll be wearing is black", so back the coat was brought. The customs of St Brigid's Eve, St John's Night and Halloween were recounted in great detail.

Mary reminded the general company of a character called "Paddy the Barrow" who would call once a month on his way from Horse and Jockey, or "Jack and Dandy" as he named it. He would sell meal and potatoes for the geese and pigs and would push a barrow of clothes before him. His clothes were covered in patches, and his trousers sported so many of them "you could say there were six trousers in it." He was a knight of the road, who would sleep in a bed of straw in the outhouse, and when he died, they found 230 half sovereigns in his pockets.

Talk continued with reminiscences of Pat Morrough, Mick Tomásin and Mickey Tuesday, who might be called Mickey Wednesday in Boherlahan!

On 3rd July 1985, Katie Ryan celebrated her 94th birthday at her home in Dualla, and on that day, she sang for her guests the grand old song *Erin go Bráth*.

> "Oh land of the west, fairest gem of the sea,
> The home of the brave though not of the free,
> Ever lovely though fallen, oh who would not draw,
> The last drop of his life's blood for Erin go Bráth."

Her sister, Mary, contributed to the gaiety of the occasion with her great rendition of *"An Irish Boy"*.

> "Oh I am an Irish boy

And my heart is full of joy
And I owe my birth to famous Cashel city
I can handle well a twig
I can dance a reel or jig
I can sing a verse of any native ditty."

Katie, not to be outdone, performs her famous tongue twister. "It must be said quick" she instructs.

"Come in and sit down and look out, and don't be outside standing
up looking in at the people inside sitting down looking out."

When the laughter had died down, she was asked to sing the Christmas song she loved, and, she lifted her sweet voice and began,

"It was Christmas Eve in London and the snow lay on the ground,
Through the window of a cottage I was passing came a sound,
Someone played an old piano, as the hands stole o'er the keys
I was taken back in fancy to my home across the seas."

This was followed by *Rory Ó Mac Rory* which tells of a trip to Killorglin Fair, where the Kerry boys were dancing, but none could better the brave Rory Ó.

As the recording came to a close, the laughter and conversation continued unabated, and as I listened, I could only bless Maura O'Brien's foresight all those years ago, when she took down her recorder and committed to tape the grand old voices of her beloved family members at their home in Dualla, Co Tipperary.